THE ORANGE GROVE

Tom Jacobson

BROADWAY PLAY PUBLISHING INC
New York
www.broadwayplaypub.com
info@broadwayplaypub.com

THE ORANGE GROVE
© Copyright 2017 Tom Jacobson

Cover photo compliments of Playwrights' Arena

First edition: December 2017
I S B N: 978-0-88145-748-3

Book design: Marie Donovan
Page make-up: Adobe InDesign
Typeface: Palatino

THE ORANGE GROVE opened 22 January 2004 at Lutheran Church of The Master in Los Angeles, produced by Playwrights' Arena (Jon Lawrence Rivera, Artistic Director). The cast and creative contributors were:

PETER TURNER .... Tom Beyer
LARRY YOSHITOSHI .... Peter James Smith
LOTTIE BERMAN .... Rebecca Metz
YOLANDA OLAFSON .... Emily Kosloski
VERONICA RICHARDS .... Bonita Friedericy
GUSTAFINA LIEDTKE .... Mary Cobb
PASTOR .... Kevin Crowley
SIMON CARPENTER .... Joshua Wolf Coleman
NORBERT BRANMOE .... Don Oscar Smith

Director .... Jessica Kubzansky
Set/costume design .... Barbara Lempel
Lighting design .... Kathi O'Donohue
Sound design .... Veronika Vortel

CHARACTERS & SETTING

PETER TURNER, *30s-40s, an organist*

LARRY YOSHITOSHI, *30s, a software expert (sings bass)*

LOTTIE BERMAN, *30s-40s, the church office manager (sings soprano)*

YOLANDA OLAFSON, *20s, an aspiring opera singer (sings soprano)*

VERONICA RICHARDS, *40s-60s, a nurse (sings alto)*

GUSTAFINA LIEDTKE, *90s, a widow (sings alto)*

PASTOR, *40s-60s, a genial tenor*

SIMON CARPENTER, *20s-40s, a homeless tenor*

NORBERT BRANMOE, *50s-60s, the congregational president (sings bass)*

The action takes place in the choir room or sanctuary of Orange Grove Lutheran Church in Los Angeles. The time is 2004.

If the set is a choir room, it may be very stark, with only chairs and a piano. If the set is a church sanctuary, then it should include pews, a piano (and/or organ), and stairs leading to a chancel with an altar. The most optimal staging is to perform the play environmentally in the sanctuary of an actual church.

Special thanks to Tina Appel, Christian Boyce,
Barbara Browning, Arne Foss, Emily Jackson-Yano,
Sara McGah, Reverend Robert Sterling Richards,
Ken Roehrs, Reverend John Rollefson, Ruth Rollefson,
James Taulbee, Ty Woodward, David York, and
everyone at Lutheran Church of the Master

ACT ONE

(With the houselights still on in a church sanctuary or choir rehearsal room, PETER TURNER, 30s-40s, comes in carrying a sheaf of music and wearing a light jacket. He sits at the piano, sorts the music meticulously, and selects a few pieces. He plays a medley of For All the Saints, Three Kings *from Mendelsohn's* Elijah, What Child is This?, *and* Thine is the Glory. *As he concentrates on his music, a number of other people quietly enter the room. VERONICA RICHARDS, 40s-60s, wearing a nurse uniform, comes in carrying a Tupperware container of homemade treats and a bottle of communion wine. Just passing through, she disappears, jingling a set of keys. Overlapping her entrance, SIMON, 20s-40s, comes in from another direction. He is rather scruffy and wears several layers of clothing—none of them particularly clean—and starts shedding them while standing rather close to the piano and staring intently at PETER, who studiously ignores him as he plays. LOTTIE BERMAN, 30s-40s, comes in carrying a recorder case and a few pieces of paper. She looks around, then almost bumps into NORBERT BRANMOE, 50s-60s, as he enters and she tries to leave.)*

NORBERT: Excuse me—

LOTTIE: *(With a nod toward PETER)* Shhh!

NORBERT: Oh, right, sorry—

LOTTIE: Shhhh!!

(LOTTIE leaves. NORBERT goes to the lighting controls [or switch] and starts dimming the house lights as well as turning on additional lights and adjusting them. LARRY YOSHITOSHI, 30s, comes in with music. When PETER sees him, he stops playing.)

LARRY: *(On cell phone)* You shoulda got a Mac. Gotta go. I'm late.

PETER: *(Slight Oklahoma accent)* Late!

LARRY: Traffic—Santa Monica Boulevard—

SIMON: Mr Turner—

PETER: Three minutes before the full rehearsal—

LARRY: I practiced on Sunday, but it's been a few days—

SIMON: Mr Turner—

PETER: Simon, we need to rehearse Larry's solo, and he's late—

LARRY: *(Overlapping)* —Late, I'm late. But I'm ready—

SIMON: Just wanted you to know your car is fine.

PETER:	LARRY:
Oh…good.	Hey, nice haircut.
	SIMON:
Thanks. Yours is too short—*again*.	I been watching it and it's fine.

PETER: 'Preciate it. Why don't you sit and listen to Larry? He's been *practicing*.

LARRY: Yeah, well, we'll see. Need to do this quick so Yolanda will be surprised—

(PETER starts to play and LARRY gets ready to sing. SIMON stands there, staring for a moment longer. LARRY sings O God Our Help in Ages Past in a strained, nervous tenor voice that is somehow charming in its naiveté. SIMON gets bored, sits down and organizes the clothes he shed.

While LARRY *sings,* NORBERT *continues to play with the lights.* LOTTIE *comes back in and assembles her recorder.* VERONICA *passes through jingling her keys but without the treats or the wine.* LOTTIE *hands* VERONICA *her papers as she passes by.)*

VERONICA: Oh, Lottie, the bulletin—thank you—

LOTTIE: Shhh!

*(*VERONICA *takes the papers and starts to leave, almost running into* PASTOR, *40s-60s, and* GUSTAFINA, *90s, as they come in.* PASTOR *wears clerical garb.)*

VERONICA: Pastor! Welcome back!

PETER:	SIMON:	PASTOR:
Just in time for rehearsal!	Oh, Father, could you—	Hello, everybody!

*(*VERONICA *leaves.* PASTOR *waves at* LOTTIE, *who waves back with her recorder.* SIMON *immediately goes to* PASTOR *and whispers in his ear.* PASTOR *digs in his pocket and gives* SIMON *a little money.* GUSTAFINA *takes her seat.* SIMON *leaves.* LARRY *returns to singing.)*

LOTTIE: *(A warning)* Yolanda!

*(*LARRY *immediately stops singing, and* PETER *stops playing.* YOLANDA, *an attractive soprano in her 20s, comes in wearing a backpack.)*

YOLANDA: Pastor, *comment allez-vous?*

PASTOR: *Tres bien, et tu?*

*(*LARRY *hides his music and goes to* YOLANDA. LOTTIE *practices on her recorder.)*

YOLANDA: *Ça va.* That's all my French. How was Provence?

PASTOR: *Tres jolie!* And at Taizé we learned a brand new liturgy. But it's terrific to be home. *Bon soir,* Larry!

LARRY:
(*Helping* YOLANDA
with her backpack)
Bone sewer, Pastor.

NORBERT:
(*Approaching* PASTOR)
Are you jet-lagged?
I always get so worn
out coming back from
Minnesota—

PASTOR: That sounded wonderful!

YOLANDA:
What did?
(*Struggling out of the
backpack.*)
Larry—ow!

PASTOR:
Not at all! Just walking in,
seeing this, all of you—
(*Tears in his eyes*)
C'est manifique. Tres bien,
oui, tres bien. Pardonez-
moi—

LARRY: My French.

(PASTOR *leaves, almost bumping into* SIMON *as* SIMON
enters.)

YOLANDA: Your French is unpardonable.

NORBERT:
He really shouldn't—

YOLANDA:
Gustafina, how are you?

SIMON:
Thanks, Father!
(*To the others.*)
Father gave me—
look, he gave me—
(*Dashes out*)

GUSTAFINA:
Sehr gut.

NORBERT:
He's a pastor, not a father!

YOLANDA: Oh, don't make me do French *and* German
tonight! (*Dashes out*)

LARRY: (*Following* YOLANDA) Yolanda—!

NORBERT: (*Leaving with* LARRY) He doesn't have that
kind of money—neither does the church—

(*Everyone has left except* LOTTIE, GUSTAFINA *and* PETER.)

PETER: *Guten abend,* Frau Liedtke.

GUSTAFINA: *(German accent)* How are you, Peter?

PETER: I could have sworn there was a choir here a minute ago. No one takes All Saints Sunday seriously but me.

GUSTAFINA: I am on time.

PETER: *Ja, sehr Deutsch!*

GUSTAFINA: Ach, your German is terrible!

VERONICA: *(Bustling back in with papers and her keys)* So, Peter, did you hear about the school?

PETER: What'd they break now?

VERONICA: Their lease. They're leaving.

PETER: Leaving!?

VERONICA: After Christmas.

PETER: In the middle of the school year?

VERONICA: They found a facility with handicap access. Methodist.

PETER: But…doesn't their rent pay for about a third of our budget?

GUSTAFINA: Half!

(Concerned, LOTTIE stops practicing her recorder.)

VERONICA:	PETER:
A little more than that. *(Handing LOTTIE the papers)* I edited the psalm. It was way too long.	Somebody shoulda managed that relationship better.

PETER: How can we get another school mid-year?	LOTTIE: You edited God?

VERONICA: We can't. And we'd have to meet A D A requirements anyway, at least forty thousand dollars.

PETER:
Does Pastor even know?

(YOLANDA *comes in,*
followed by SIMON.)

GUSTAFINA:
Ja. Talked about it in the
car all the way here.

YOLANDA:
Simon, I can't give you any
money.

PETER:
I thought he seemed more
choked up than normal.

SIMON:
I don't want money.

VERONICA:
I'll start the coffee.
(Leaves)

YOLANDA:
Ask Pastor for money.

LARRY:
(Sticking his head in the
door)
Oo-ee-oo!
(Disappears)

SIMON:
(Grabbing an offering
envelope and pencil)
Your—your— autograph.

GUSTAFINA:
(Startled)
Mein Gott!

YOLANDA:
My autograph!?

SIMON:
What was that?

LOTTIE:
(At the same time)
Her autograph?!

LARRY:
(Sticks his head in again.)
Oo-ee-oo!

SIMON:
Before you go off to the
opera and get famous—

YOLANDA: *(Signing the envelope with the pencil)* I could
write you a whole novel before that happens. Peter,
can we practice my solo after?

PETER:
Won't be an after till we
get started.

YOLANDA:
Oh, Larry, stop.

LARRY: *(Coming in)* I'm a llama. When I was in Big Sur last year I heard llamas greeting each other, and that's what it sounded like. *(Makes llama ears with his fingers.)* Oo-ee-oo! How was the workshop?

YOLANDA:	SIMON:
Just exercises all day, no real singing. I'm so past that.	*(Trying to get her attention)* I sweat too much. Once I had to leave a party cause I dripped in the punch. I don't go to parties now.

LARRY: You have to work if you want—

YOLANDA: Like I need a lecture after eight hours of "ma me mi mo moo, ma me mi mo moo."

LARRY: The Master Chorale called again. Why haven't you—?

YOLANDA: Larry, I'm a soloist! Not—

LARRY: *(Making llama ears)* Oo-ee-oo!

(SIMON also makes llama ears.)

SIMON & LARRY: Oo-ee-oo!

SIMON, LOTTIE & LARRY: Oo-ee-oo!

YOLANDA: Honestly!

PETER:	NORBERT:
Will the llamas please take their seats? I'd like to get us out of here by nine.	*(Coming back in with PASTOR and taking a seat)*
LARRY:	—So I'm planning on running a speaker wire out
Yeah, we need to get started.	to the narthex so mothers with crying babies can
PASTOR:	listen to the sermon—
Wonderful, Norbert.	

LOTTIE: If there were any babies…

YOLANDA: We only have one soprano.

LOTTIE: More than enough.

SIMON: Yolanda, Larry's got a surprise for you.

YOLANDA: A surprise? Really?

LARRY: It's nothing. *Simon!*

YOLANDA: Larry, that's so sweet.

PETER: People, people, please.

(Holding up an anthem. Everyone digs through their folders for the anthem.)

PETER: I know you think you know the anthem cause it's a familiar hymn, but I want it in parts and it's not as easy as it seems. Especially for the men.

PASTOR: Except for the tenors, of course.

SIMON: We got it perfect.   LOTTIE: Tenors!

PETER: Faith like a mustardseed. Starting with verse two, men only, please. *(Plays brief introduction.)*

(LOTTIE and YOLANDA whisper to each other and giggle as:)

MEN: *(Singing, not very well)*
Oh, blest communion, fellowship divine
We feebly struggle, they in glory shine
Yet all are one within your grand design
Alleluia! Alleluia!

PETER: Gentlemen, you've done a marvelous job of suiting sound to sense—

LARRY: We're in glory shining?

PETER: No, feebly struggling. Let's hear the tenors on that line.

(Singing as PETER plays:)

PASTOR & SIMON: We feebly struggle—

PETER: Without me this time.

(Singing without PETER playing:)

PASTOR & SIMON: We feebly struggle—

PETER: You're a little under pitch on the C sharp. Try raising your eyebrows.

PASTOR & SIMON: (*Singing with exaggeratedly raised eyebrows*)
We feebly struggle—

PETER: Better. Basses, same line.

PASTOR: Only better? Not perfect? We *are* tenors.

PETER: Yes, but don't give up hope. Basses.

LARRY & NORBERT: (*Singing,* LARRY *enthusiastically,* NORBERT *quietly.*)
We feebly struggle, they in glory shine—

PETER: Larry, a little more feeble, Norbert a little less. Can you open your mouth a bit more?

NORBERT: (*With a very small mouth*) No.

PETER: No?

NORBERT: I have a Norwegian jaw. My dentist told me it's the smallest bite he's ever seen. Very limited range of movement.

YOLANDA: I'm Norwegian and I have a big bite. (*Demonstrates*)

NORBERT:	LOTTIE:
Oh, no. Mine's unusually small.	That's for sure.

(*Demonstrates*)

PASTOR: It's a very polite bite, Norbert.

NORBERT: I don't have what you'd call a leadership mouth. I'm more suited to be vice president than president of the congregation—heh, heh—

PETER: All of the men, please, same place.

MEN: *(Singing.* PASTOR *hits a very sour note.)*
We feebly struggle, they in glory shine—

*(*LARRY *breaks up with laughter.)*

SIMON:	YOLANDA:	LOTTIE:
Feeble!	That was scary.	What was that?

NORBERT: Heh, heh—that was definitely a struggle.

PASTOR: I thought I was much better that time.

PETER: It was a bold mistake, a proud Lutheran sour note—

PASTOR: Oh, that's a *treble* clef!

LARRY: Sorry, speaking of struggle, I just had an idea about the school.

NORBERT:	PETER:
I've been thinking about that, too.	Wouldn't the council meeting be a better—?

LARRY: Rather than chase after the money to bring us up to handicap standards, why don't we sell the property and merge with another congregation, say whatchacallit in Santa Monica—?

GUSTAFINA: Merge?

NORBERT:	PETER:
You mean Mount Olive?	People, people—

PASTOR: The folks at Mount Olive'd never come here—their building's much newer than ours.

LARRY: No, if *we* sell—the land alone—we're sitting on at least a million dollars—we could create an endowment for a larger, stronger congregation—

GUSTAFINA:	SIMON:
Sell the church?	What's an endowment?

*(*PETER *starts noodling on the piano.)*

LARRY: I keep telling you we're really naïve about
money, not asking for pledges for the coming year—

LOTTIE:
That's what we do at my
temple—pledges—

YOLANDA:
Aren't we here to *sing*?

NORBERT:
It's called a faith budget.

PASTOR:
The Lord will provide.

LARRY:
It's bad—stewardship—
that's the word you use,
right, Pastor? We could
do some good with that
money. Isn't that what
churches are supposed
to do—good?

YOLANDA:
Larry, please!

PASTOR:
Let's not forget we're at
choir rehearsal—

PETER: Yes, oo-ee-oo, choir!

PASTOR: Larry, you know how many Lutherans it takes
to change a light bulb?

LARRY: How many?

EVERYONE: *(Except* LARRY. *In mock horror and
astonishment—it's an old joke of* PASTOR'*s.)* Change??!!

LARRY: Just a suggestion.

PETER: I suggest we hear the women on verse two.

YOLANDA:
Please!

LOTTIE:
Who?

PETER: Oh, blest communion.

GUSTAFINA: Where?

PETER: Verse *two*. Shall we? Do let's.

(Singing as PETER *plays:)*

WOMEN & PASTOR:
Oh, blest communion, fellowship divine—

(LARRY *snorts. Everyone looks at him.)*

PETER: The women are sounding frighteningly postmenopausal.

PASTOR: Oh, did you say just the women? *Pardonez moi.*

(LARRY *cracks up.)*

PETER: This time with estrogen.

WOMEN: *(Singing, with* LOTTIE *flat and* GUSTAFINA *starting each line early.)*
Oh, blest communion, fellowship divine
We feebly struggle, they in glory shine

(YOLANDA *glares at* GUSTAFINA. LARRY *giggles more.)*

WOMEN: Yet all are one within your grand design
Alleluia! Alleluia!

(LARRY *is laughing silently but very hard. He's almost drooling.* PASTOR *starts to giggle as well.)*

YOLANDA:	LARRY:
Larry, honestly!	*(Trying to stifle his laughter)* I'm sorry. I'm sorry.

PETER:	PASTOR:
Lottie, I think you're a wee bit flat.	I can't help it, either!

SIMON:	NORBERT:
I don't know why but she sounds terrible.	Hoo-boy!

(LARRY *makes a strange stifled-laughter noise, almost a choking sound.* PASTOR *cracks up.)*

YOLANDA: Try coming down on top of the note rather than scooping up to it. And *smile.*

LOTTIE: *(Chilly)* Oh. Thank you.

YOLANDA: Larry, it's *not funny.*

LARRY: *(Barely able to speak)* Sorry.

PETER: And Gustafina—

(No response. PETER speaks louder.)

PETER: Frau Liedtke!

GUSTAFINA: Yes?

(YOLANDA leaves.)

PETER: I appreciate your leadership in coming in even a little earlier than everyone else—

GUSTAFINA: Thank you. My daughter gave it to me for Christmas last year.

PETER: *(Louder)* Promptness is certainly a virtue, but watch me so we all start together, all right?

GUSTAFINA: All night?

PETER: *(Very loud)* Just watch me, please. Let's try it with everybody—

(GUSTAFINA takes out her hearing aid and bangs it against the seat, then puts it back in. At the same time, SIMON waves his hand as if to clear the air.)

PETER: Yes, Simon?

SIMON: One of the tenors made boom gas.

(PASTOR looks embarrassed, as he's the only other tenor.)

PETER: Think of it as the peace that passeth understanding. Everyone. Where'd Yolanda go?

YOLANDA: *(Coming back with a glass of water)* My chords were dry. Better to have water than—

GUSTAFINA: *(A small gasp)* Gretchen!

YOLANDA: Gretchen who?

PASTOR: No, Gustafina, it's only Yolanda.

(As LOTTIE giggles:)

YOLANDA: *Only* Yolanda?

(LARRY *and* PASTOR *confer in whispers.*)

GUSTAFINA: Oh, my dear! I'm so sorry. Just now you looked like my grand-daughter Gretchen. Gave me the shivers—she died in a car accident six years ago. Where are my pills?

PETER:	NORBERT:
(*Going to* GUSTAFINA) They do look alike, don't they?	She and her parents didn't come to church.

GUSTAFINA:	YOLANDA:
She was very pretty, like you.	Oh, I remember her. She sang, right?

SIMON: Nobody's pretty as Yolanda.

PETER:	NORBERT:
She played piano.	A very pretty girl.

GUSTAFINA: And Peter was her music teacher. Back when he was in graduate school.

LOTTIE: Oh, you finished? Congratulations.

PETER: No, I'm still at U S C.

YOLANDA:	SIMON:
They let you stay that long?	He's never gonna graduate.

GUSTAFINA:	PASTOR:
(*To* PETER) Sometimes it's so painful even to see you at choir. (*To* YOLANDA) And tonight you were almost like her ghost. A doppelganger— you know the German word?	(*To* LARRY) I don't care about property values!

YOLANDA: No.

LARRY: Shall we try verse one, all of us? I know the tune.

PETER: Ah, maybe that's what we need—the unison part! It's getting late and we're not even through our first anthem.

EVERYONE: *(Singing. Very boldly unison. It sounds pretty good.)*
For all the saints, who from their labors rest
All who by faith before the world confessed

(As they sing, VERONICA comes in with her keys, sits down, pulls out her music and prepares to sing.)

EVERYONE:
Your name, O Jesus, be forever blest
Alleluia! Alleluia!

VERONICA: *(Opens her mouth to sing, just as they've finished.)* Oh! I'm sorry. Coffee's ready.

PETER: We haven't quite earned our break yet.

NORBERT:	VERONICA:
I could use some coffee, 'cause my throat gets quite dry. *(Puts a cough drop in his mouth)* As you get older, you don't produce as much phlegm.	And there are some lemon ginger coconut bars—

PASTOR:	LOTTIE:
While we're on break—	I don't have phlegm. It's not ladylike.

PETER: We're not on break—!

PASTOR: I'd like everyone to think about an idea I had. With the school gone, we'll need to save some money, and I was thinking—

NORBERT & PETER: No!

PASTOR: Now, wait a minute. You don't know what I was going to propose.

(They stare at PASTOR *for a moment.)*

PASTOR: I was thinking that perhaps we could budget for a little less salary for me next year—

NORBERT & PETER: No!

VERONICA: Pastor, you do this every year.

NORBERT: Heh, heh. And every year the Council says no.

VERONICA: And if Fred Briscoe were here, he'd give you a raise for having the nerve to propose such a thing!

LARRY:	SIMON:
He *is* here.	When I was a baby I used to pretend to be dead to freak my parents out. A tiny baby!

NORBERT: That's right!

PETER: Under the altar—

YOLANDA: What?

LARRY: I found a bunch of little white boxes under there when I was helping Norbert install the sound system. I opened one up before I saw the label—cremated human remains!

LOTTIE: Ew! Is that what those are?

PASTOR:	YOLANDA:
Doris didn't want to keep dusting him at home.	Larry, ishda!

NORBERT: So, Pastor, if you don't stop talking like that, we'll have to bring Fred out to testify.

YOLANDA: If you want to save money, don't hire that liturgical dance troupe for Pentecost.

VERONICA:	SIMON:
Oh, we have to!	That was stupid!
(Making liturgical dance movements)	
I thought it was beautiful.	LOTTIE:
	That was Pastor's idea.

LARRY: It's not just saving a penny here or there or finding forty thousand for an A D A renovation. Any time I make practical suggestions for stabilizing finances or increasing attendance, everybody tells me why we can't—

PETER: People...

NORBERT: We'll find the money. We always do. We bought the new organ seventeen years ago and raised the hundred and sixty thousand dollars in just eighteen months!

PETER: People...

PASTOR:	LOTTIE:
That's a big reason we can't merge with with another church.	A big waste, if you ask me, a congregation this small.

VERONICA:	NORBERT:
The organ's built to last fifty years.	It's not a waste!

(PETER wanders out.)

NORBERT:	YOLANDA:
It has fifteen ranks of pipes, which is a lot for a sanctuary this size. Our organ donors wanted a real pipe organ,	Excuse me, but Peter's *leaving.*

not one of those
electric digital ones.

LARRY:	SIMON:
Like I said—just a	Hey, where'd Mr Turner
suggestion.	go?

VERONICA: I don't think we're going anywhere. When
did your husband found Orange Grove Lutheran,
Gustafina?

GUSTAFINA: Nineteen and forty-four, right after his
ordination. His first church—his only church! This was
just an orange grove then. The oranges were so sweet.
We still had ten trees. After the education building,
there were three, but there came some fungus.

LOTTIE: Now there's only one old tree left.

LARRY: Forget I ever mentioned merging—!

PASTOR: We don't need to think about that. Not yet,
anyway.

(PETER *wanders back in, eating an orange.*)

LARRY:	PETER:
It just seems like a	Yecch! Sour!
realistic approach—	
given the upkeep	
required here.	

NORBERT: I take care of maintenance. A merger's giving
up, like huddling together against the cold, unchristian
world. A last desperate—

VERONICA:	YOLANDA:
Peter, don't we need to	Okay, everybody, Peter's
practice? Isn't this	back.
the anthem for Sunday?	

PETER: Oh. You think?

PASTOR: I think it's coming along very nicely. At least—

LARRY & PASTOR: —In the tenor section.

(LARRY *cracks up.*)

PETER: Let's try the third verse. Different words, but the same harmony as verse two. *(Gives pitches)*

EVERYONE: *(In harmony and a capella. It sounds pretty good.)*
The golden evening brightens in the west
Soon, soon to faithful warriors comes their rest
Sweet is the calm of paradise the blest

(SIMON *starts waving his hand to indicate personal gas.*)

EVERYONE: Alleluia! Alleluia!

YOLANDA: *(To* LOTTIE*)* Smile!	(GUSTAFINA *takes her pills out of her purse and gets ready to take one.*)

VERONICA: Simon, stop that!

SIMON: It's bad!

PETER: You sounded very good that time, now—

SIMON: I'm gonna have to go outside—

PETER: No!

(GUSTAFINA *signals for a sip of* YOLANDA'*s water to take her pill.* YOLANDA *gives her the water.*)

VERONICA: Simon, behave—

SIMON: It's not me—it's Father!

VERONICA: Simon, that's enough!

PASTOR: Veronica, it's all right. Simon, sit down—

SIMON: Does anybody have any—just a little—today's not been a good day—

NORBERT: Pastor already gave you too much—	VERONICA: You're just trying to get attention.

SIMON: *(Grabs* GUSTAFINA's *pills)* I am not. *(Puts all the pills in his mouth at once)*

GUSTAFINA: My pills!

LARRY: Hey, you might wanna spit those out.

(SIMON grabs the water from YOLANDA *and swallows some with the pills.)*

NORBERT: What are they?

VERONICA:	GUSTAFINA:
Blood pressure, who knows what could—	Veronica, I need those!

SIMON: They don't do anything. See?

VERONICA:	PETER:
Gustafina, I'll refill your prescription first thing tomorrow.	People...people!

PASTOR: Perhaps now we've earned our break.

NORBERT: A little—

VERONICA:	GUSTAFINA:
Coffee! There's coffee in the coffee room.	Treats?

LARRY:	LOTTIE:
And cookies?	What kind of treats?

VERONICA:	GUSTAFINA:
Bars—lemon ginger coconut.	*(Leaving)* Ginger—good for the digestion.

YOLANDA:	VERONICA:
Homemade?	*(Leaving)* Oh, I forgot the cream. Does anyone want lemonade instead of coffee?

LARRY:
(Leaving)
I didn't have dessert.

SIMON:	NORBERT:
(Starting to leave)	*(Starting to leave)*

PETER: I want lemonade.   I could use a
Maybe we should   little—
take—

YOLANDA:	PETER:
(Leaving)	—A break.

Larry, not too many—

PASTOR: Wait, Simon, maybe Peter will go over the trio
with us. Norbert—

LOTTIE: Pastor, I'm almost done with the bulletin. I just
need you to fill in the Prayer of the Church.

PASTOR: After choir, Lottie.

LOTTIE: And can we cut out the Children's Sermon
since we haven't had children for the last four months?

PASTOR: If we stop having it, they most certainly won't
come.

LOTTIE: Never mind, then. *(She goes out.)*

NORBERT: Do you want to do the trio? Nothing wrong
with starting early.

PETER: It's only October. Christmas isn't for two
months yet.

SIMON: The one with all the oohs?

LARRY:And you've done it for the last four years.

PASTOR: Maybe this year we'll get it right.

SIMON: NORBERT:
Let's do it. I remember it.   I don't think I have my
But can I get lemonade   music.
first?

PASTOR: I'll share. Simon, why don't you have lemonade after?

(Defeated, PETER *gets out the music I Wonder as I Wander.)*

NORBERT: Oh, Pastor, I had another idea. What about the Lutheran high school? Aren't you on that committee for the synod? They could use our education building or even tear it down—and we could finally get some good parking built—

*(*NORBERT *notices that* PETER *is seated at the piano staring at them expectantly.* NORBERT *shuts up and gets in position.* PETER *plays.)*

SIMON: *(Singing beautifully)*
I wonder as I wander out under the sky
How Jesus our savior did come down to die
For poor lowly people like you and like I
I wonder as I wander out under the sky.

(While SIMON *sings verses two through four while* PASTOR *and* NORBERT *accompany him with oohs,* LOTTIE *appears in warmer [California winter] clothes and changes the lights.* VERONICA *and* LARRY *appear, also in warmer clothes. They each add a Christmas decoration to the set. After they've added their decorations, they perform a mock liturgical dance behind the men as they sing. During the dance,* YOLANDA *[also in warmer clothes] adds a few decorations [with help from* LOTTIE*] then takes her seat.* GUSTAFINA *comes in wearing winter clothes and takes her seat as well. By the end of the song and the dance,* LOTTIE, GUSTAFINA *and even* PETER *are enjoying a good laugh.)*

SIMON: I wonder as I wander out under the sky
How Jesus our savior did come down to die
For poor lowly people like you and like I
I wonder as I wander out under the sky.

PETER: Good, good—it's only mid-December—we've still got ten days till Christmas, so there's time to polish.

YOLANDA:
Larry, for heaven's sake!

PETER & LARRY:
What?

SIMON:
Do you ever worry that you're going to suddenly lose your mind and eat something gross off the sidewalk?

YOLANDA: Oh, nothing, he was just—

VERONICA: *(Starting to leave)* It was liturgical dance! I hope you appreciated it. We've been practicing for weeks!

PETER: Thank you everyone for a wonderful rehearsal.

(SIMON starts to run out.)

PETER: Wait, Simon. Pastor?

PASTOR: *(As everyone bows their heads.)* Gracious God, thank you for this evening when we can join together to praise your name and enjoy each other's company. Bless our preparations for the celebration of the birth of your Son. Please guide us safely home and watch over those who have no place to go this night. In Jesus' name we pray—

EVERYONE: Amen.

(Everyone prepares to leave, gathering coats, etc.)

YOLANDA: Larry, I'll see you in the car. *(She leaves.)*

SIMON: Anybody seen my toothbrush?
(Disappears.)

NORBERT:
Veronica, before you run off—

PASTOR:
Happy Hanukkah, Lottie.

VERONICA:
I can't talk long, Norbert— I'm taking some blankets to

LOTTIE:
Merry Christmas, everyone.

PETER:
Happy Hanukkah.

LARRY:
(Grinning)
Gonna invite your
grandmother to the
Christmas Eve service?

LOTTIE:
She still doesn't know
I work here.

PASTOR:
Best office manager
we've ever had.

She'd die if she knew
Once I was with her
at Century City and
Mrs Liedtke came up
and started talking to
me about church.
Afterwards my
grandmother said,
"that woman must
be crazy."

LARRY:
Do you need any more

the community center.

NORBERT:
I'll make it quick—you
know I'm the chair of the
nominating committee for
council—

VERONICA:
Is my term up? Of course
I'll go on council again—

NORBERT:
No, it's not up till next
year, but I don't know if
you know I've decided
being president of the
congregation is just a little
too much for me,
overwhelming, you
know—

VERONICA:
Gustafina, do you have
a ride?

GUSTAFINA:
Ja, Pastor's taking me.

help with the office
software?

LOTTIE:
Fine for now.

LARRY:
You're not still retyping
the council minutes after
I email them to you?

LOTTIE:
Oh, no.

LARRY:
Good, cause next I wanna
teach you how to update
the webpage.

LOTTIE:
Isn't that awfully...
technical?

LARRY:
A little. But I'll show you.
Not to brag, but I got the
website date to change at
sundown every night,
to make it more biblical.

LOTTIE:
And Jewish.

NORBERT:
So I was wondering—
I know you might not have
a lot of energy for it now—

VERONICA:
Oh, I'm fine—

NORBERT:
You do half of this stuff
anyway, so I was
wondering if you'd be
interested in being
president of the
congregation come
January.

VERONICA:
Oh, no.

NORBERT:
I understand, with the
chemotherapy and all—

VERONICA:
It's not that. It just
wouldn't be right for
me to be out front like
that.

NORBERT:
But I'm thinking it's time
we had a woman as
president—

LARRY:
So the Genesis verse
changes for each day
of the week—on Sunday
it's "And he rested
on the seventh day from
all his work which he had
made."

LOTTIE:
That's where it stops
being Jewish.

LARRY:
Pastor, why is that?
Why is our Sabbath
different from the Jews'?

PASTOR:
Sunday is the day of
resurrection, a new world,
starting over—Easter
changed everything—

LARRY:
I see. Well, anyway,
I emailed a friend who
gave me this fancy
algorithm to change
the date automatically,
but it used up too much
memory, so I found a
different way. I also
figured out, and this

VERONICA:
Gustafina, what would you
think of that—a woman as
president of the
congregation?

GUSTAFINA:
Ach, my husband would
rise up from his grave!
Never while he was pastor!

VERONICA:
See, Norbert?

NORBERT:
Well, you can't fault me for
trying.

VERONICA:
You should stay president,
Norbert. You're doing a
great job!

NORBERT:
Oh, no. What with the
school and all, I don't
know if I'm up to the
challenge of the next year.

is pretty cool, how to
change the background
color of the website to
match the—
whatchacallit—liturgical
color of the church year.
So if you look at it now
it's blue for Advent, but
it will change to white
for Christmas in a week—
all automatically, I only
had to set it up this year
and it will do it by itself
in the future.

VERONICA:
I'll stay on the evangelism
committee and the
education committee
though. I've got some ideas
for visitor follow up.

LOTTIE:
Neat. Excuse me, I've got
to go light some candles.
Pastor, any luck finding
the missing offering?

NORBERT:
That's very important,
very important.

PASTOR:
Not yet, I'm afraid.
That's wonderful, Larry
I know you're busy
with your business—

LARRY:
(Shrugging modestly)
Hey.

(LOTTIE starts searching
for the lost offering.)

VERONICA:
We can't just send a note
once and expect them to
come back. We've got to be
more aggressive, especially
with the neighborhood
changing—

GUSTAFINA:
No families any more.

PASTOR:
—So it's great that you
can take the time for the   VERONICA:
website. It looks better   So transitory. I'm going to
than any other Lutheran   make it a goal to have fifty
website I've seen—   people as our average
                                    attendance next year.

PETER:
That one with the
revolving crosses!
Can't you make ours
do that, Larry?   NORBERT:
                                    That's ambitious. Very
                                    good.

PASTOR: I'm so glad you joined the church. I remember
when your dad was gardener here and he used to
bring you with him. I always felt bad—

LARRY: It was all very mysterious to me, since Dad
didn't want us raised in any religion. But now I think
of him every time I come here *(Overhearing* VERONICA*)*
Fifty doesn't seem ambitious to me. Why do we have
so few?

YOLANDA: *(Coming back in)* Larry, I have an audition in
the morning.

NORBERT: There are too many Lutheran churches in
L A. Used to need more because eighty years ago they
conducted services in different languages—

GUSTAFINA: NORBERT: VERONICA:
One church in   All those Scanda- Norwegian,
German—   hoovians—   Swedish—

PASTOR: —Kind of a Babel. But when the Evangelical
Lutheran Church in America was formed—

PASTOR	NORBERT
—By the merger in 1988—	With everybody speaking English—

LARRY: I get it. Too many churches and not enough people in 'em. And it goes without saying, not enough offering come Sunday. Hey, a developer I know told me this property is worth at least a million and a half. He's even interested—

LOTTIE: Well, here it is! *(Produces an offering plate—full of money—from under* PASTOR'*s seat.)* Has this been here since Sunday?

PASTOR:	VERONICA:	PETER:
(Taking it from LOTTIE*)* I guess so. Good work, Lottie. *(Accidentally drops the offering plate, scattering money.)* Oop.	Norbert, what about Larry?

NORBERT:
Larry? He doesn't have time—

VERONICA:
Let me talk to Pastor. | Oh, for heaven's sake! |

LOTTIE:
Oh, Pastor!

PETER: Now we know what happened to the music fund.

(Everyone helps pick up the money and put it back in the offering plate.)

LOTTIE:
This is serious! Now our deposit won't balance—
worse than the counters

usually do, and they're bad enough. We've had checks bouncing all over the place lately, almost completely gone through the savings. And this has been just sitting out since Sunday—all kinds of people wander in here all the time off the street, some of them kinda weird. I'm only a green belt, so I get nervous. I'm trying to do my job properly, but—	YOLANDA: Checks bouncing, really? NORBERT: Oh, yeah, it's getting bad.

PASTOR: Managing money doesn't seem to be one of my gifts. *(Laughs)*

LOTTIE: *(Almost muttering)* Not funny. It's not.	LARRY: Well, if anybody would listen to me about that—

VERONICA: It doesn't matter. I go over the books—

PASTOR: But I think I've talked the Schermers into a forty thousand dollar gift to cover the A D A renovations—

NORBERT: Really? That's a great step.	VERONICA: They never come.

PETER: Well, they can't sing.	GUSTAFINA: Forty thousand!

PASTOR: But they bought us the van a couple of years ago—	YOLANDA: He can, a little. But she sounds like cats mating. And she lost so much weight she looks like a sharpei.

NORBERT: Then we'd just need to find another school
tenant. But the renovation could take a while—

GUSTAFINA:
(Overlapping) It wasn't
always this scramble for
money. Back in nineteen
and fifty seven, we had
three hundred children
in Sunday School—
(To LARRY*)*
—Back when your father
was the gardener. The
choir was forty people,
and I sang solos all the
time. Back then I had a
real voice, not an old lady
voice. I know I shouldn't
be trying to sing in choir
any more, but I just can't
give it up! It's habit.

PETER:
You're voice is still lovely,
Frau Liedtke.

GUSTAFINA:
Ach, I crack and croak—

LARRY:
No, you don't.

GUSTAFINA:
Pastor Liedtke was so
proud of Sunday School—
all those kids—

LOTTIE:
You're not gonna get your
friend the contractor again?
He always goes over
budget.

NORBERT:
We always start off too
cheap is the problem.

VERONICA:
That's cause you
underestimate to get
the project past Council.

NORBERT:
Not true. Not true.

YOLANDA:
That cement picnic table
he made looks like
Stonehenge.

*(*SIMON *comes back in
with his toothbrush.)*

SIMON:
Anybody seen my pillow?

PASTOR: You and your husband did a wonderful job of building this church.

GUSTAFINA:	SIMON:
It was such a beautiful place.	*(Producing a pillow and blanket)*
(Starts reading a book)	Here it is. And my blanket.

(SIMON makes himself an improvised bed, not quite, but almost out of sight. He lies down. The others ignore him and avoid the area.)

NORBERT: It still is. I try to keep it up. If only I'd get a bigger maintenance budget—

LOTTIE:	YOLANDA:
You always go over.	Larry, my *audition*—!

LARRY:	VERONICA:
Sorry, Yolanda. I just love hearing about how the church used to be— as a kid I was always on the periphery—	I'll be cleaning up the kitchen— *(Leaves)*

PETER:	NORBERT:
Yolanda, didn't you want to go over your solo?	And you wonder why I don't want to be President!

YOLANDA:	PASTOR
If you're going to push me about my singing, you can at least get me home at a decent hour—	Veronica shouldn't clean up alone— *(Leaves)*

(NORBERT starts puttering with the seating.)

LARRY:	NORBERT:
I'm pushing you?	I don't go over budget.

YOLANDA:	LOTTIE:
The workshop—you know—	Every time.

LARRY:
I'm paying for it is all—

YOLANDA:
Don't talk about money.
You're embarrassing me.
Oh, Peter, can we practice
real quick?

LARRY:
I don't mean to—I'm
sorry—how—?

YOLANDA:
That liturgical dance,
for one thing—

PETER:
I'm thinking we should
incorporate it into our
Easter celebration. Larry,
you don't mind wearing
a black leotard, do you?

LARRY:
I will if you will, Petey.

NORBERT:
I donate all my labor.
If more people would help
me. Larry does at least.
But I'm practically a one-
man operation on the
Property Management
Committee.

LOTTIE:
If you'd make them do a
written estimate it'd be
easier to hold down costs.

NORBERT:
This darn thing!
(Banging the seating)
Ow! Oops, it broke.

(LOTTIE giggles.
NORBERT putters more.)

YOLANDA: Peter, you're not helping! Encouraging
goofiness! That's what's wrong with this church—it's
too goofy!

PETER: We have fun, but it's very serious at the same
time—

YOLANDA: Have you ever noticed that almost everyone
here is single? There's a reason for that!

PETER:
Single people have more
time to get involved—

YOLANDA:
It's inept, even tacky—
that horrible bread cake

they always serve at special
lunches—

LARRY: Bread cake?

(LOTTIE *groans at the memory.*)

PETER: It *is* terrible. Isn't it, Frau Liedtke?

GUSTAFINA: What?

YOLANDA: First you lay out slices of white bread—
Wonder Bread, preferably—on a platter. Then
spread—I dunno—salmon spread on them. On top
of that another layer of bread. Next, a layer of cream
cheese. More bread, and this time—my favorite part—
a layer of peanut butter.

LARRY: No way!

YOLANDA: Another layer of bread and another layer of
spread. Maybe deviled ham this time. One more layer
of bread, then cover the whole thing with cream cheese
and slice vertically, so it looks like layer cake. Except
when you take a bite—

LARRY: —You have peanut butter and salmon in your
mouth—

LARRY, LOTTIE & YOLANDA: —At the same time!

YOLANDA: Whose recipe is that?

LOTTIE: It's Veronica's.

PETER: And don't say anything to her. She's very proud
of it.

LARRY:	LOTTIE:
But if it's that gross—	I don't touch it.

PETER: Well, don't say anything to her till after she's
done with her chemo at least.

LARRY:	YOLANDA:
Veronica's having	Chemo? Ishda.
chemotherapy?	

PETER: Yes, so please don't disparage—

VERONICA: *(Coming in)* Oh, good. Everybody's still here.

*(*VERONICA *passes out lots of lemon ginger coconut bars.* LOTTIE *takes some and disappears.)*

VERONICA: Take these home. I won't eat them. I'm so stupid—still baking like we had more people! Don't let me interrupt—what were you talking about?

LARRY:	YOLANDA:	PETER:
Um.	Nothing.	The...uh... Reconciling in Christ program.

*(*NORBERT *groans.)*

VERONICA: Oh, that's so important. I'm glad we're doing it.

PETER:	GUSTAFINA:
I think it's the next big schism in the Christian church.	Is it almost time to go, Veronica?

LARRY:	VERONICA:
Then maybe we oughta *not*.	Isn't Pastor taking you home, Gustafina?

PETER: Every five hundred years or so there's a issue that divides the church and almost destroys it, but ultimately makes it stronger. The fall of Rome, the break with Eastern Orthodoxy, the Reformation. Now, with women ministers and issues related to gay and lesbian people—like the Reconciling in Christ program—we're in the midst of another revolution. Every mainline protestant denomination is struggling with it.

NORBERT: I don't think we're quite ready for this one.

PETER: Not an impulsive people, us Lutherans. We've been *studying* homosexuality for the last twenty years. Much more attuned to evolution than revolution.

NORBERT: Now, I don't go for that evolution stuff.

(SIMON *gets up, apparently irritated that their noise is disturbing his sleep. But he won't admit that.*)

YOLANDA: But Norbert, weren't you some kind of scientist—an engineer—before you got—before—

VERONICA:	SIMON:
(Interrupting quickly)	Veronica, do you have
Before you retired.	any—?

YOLANDA:	VERONICA:
I mean—fossils and	No.
things—	

LARRY: Carbon dating—

NORBERT: They haven't proved that carbon dating really works. And those fossils could have been formed very recently, even faked.

PETER:	SIMON:
But *in general* Lutherans	Norbert, I wonder if you
accept evolution—	could—
sorry I brought it up.	
And I'm sorry to get on	
my soapbox about	
Reconciling in Christ,	NORBERT:
but the mainline	Sorry, nothing on me. I can
protestants need to do	give you a ride anytime,
something to distinguish	Simon. Happy to do that.
themselves from the	But no money.
pentecostals and	
fundamentalist Christians	
if they're going to survive	
the century.	

YOLANDA: And is that so important?

LARRY: Yolanda!

NORBERT: This country was founded by Protestants!
(Sputtering a little) Not Catholics, not Jews, not
Buddhists or Muslims or—all our *laws* were written by
mainline Protestants—our Constitution—

YOLANDA:	NORBERT:
But not Lutherans, I bet—	The Bill of Rights, the Declaration of Independence—

LARRY:
What about televangelism?

	SIMON:
(The others laugh.)	Yolanda, I want to get a little something to eat before bed, I mean, after choir—

VERONICA:	
Have you ever seen a Lutheran on T V?	YOLANDA:
	I already told you, Simon. I'm not in a position to
PETER:	give away money.
Not exactly telegenic. Other than Davy and Goliath.	

LARRY:	PETER:
Oh, come on. Get Petey on T V, playing his organ—	Don't call me Petey!

NORBERT: Hey, hey, keep it clean—!

LARRY: I mean—

PETER: I know what you meant, Larry.

LARRY: Sorry…Pete.

PETER: Peter!

(Suddenly there is a strange, mournful sound in the distance, like giant musical sigh or someone sitting on an accordion.)

GUSTAFINA: SIMON:
Gott in Himmel! What   Aagh! Is the church
was that?   haunted?

NORBERT: Could it be the organ?

LARRY: VERONICA:
Like that time Petey fell   Oh, I hope not!
asleep on the keys during
the sermon.

PETER: Maybe some air got trapped in a pipe and just now released. If it happens again, I'll call the organ repair guy. And I did not fall asleep!

LARRY: YOLANDA: VERONICA:
Every Sunday!   Way creepy.   Peter doesn't fall
                                       asleep.

PETER: NORBERT:
Not once!   I'd hate to think
                                    something's wrong with
                                    the organ—it's practically
                                    new.

LARRY: What was the sermon last Sunday? I bet you can't even tell me Pastor's joke at the beginning.

PETER: SIMON:
He always tells the same   I know! I know!
ones. About the little boy—

                                    VERONICA:
LARRY: Sssh, Simon. He's asking
I knew it. No idea.   Peter.

PETER: It was about preparation, advent, prepare ye the way—

LARRY: That was two weeks ago. This week was Jonah, reluctant prophets—

SIMON: Peter, I wonder, could you lend me—?

PETER:	LARRY:
Simon, you know it's not a loan, and with what I make I really can't— Larry, quit!	Asleep! I knew it! Petey!
	VERONICA: Simon, Pastor already gave you some money this evening—

SIMON: No, he didn't.

GUSTAFINA: He did, too. I saw.

PASTOR: *(Coming in)* Does everyone have a ride home?

NORBERT:	GUSTAFINA:
Pastor, did you give Simon money again?	You are taking me, Pastor?
VERONICA: If you're hungry, I can thaw out some lasagna from our last Youth Club—it's only six months old.	PASTOR: Yes, of course, unless Veronica is.
	YOLANDA: Peter, can we—?
PASTOR: Oh, I don't remember— *(Digs in his pocket)*	PETER: Yes, please!
NORBERT: Pastor, don't—	*(They rehearse What Child Is This? YOLANDA sounds beautiful. LOTTIE comes in and quietly hands VERONICA some papers.)*
SIMON: I have a job, you know. It's just not a regular job.	

PASTOR:
You take care of things here
at church.

(*Over* YOLANDA's *singing:*)

SIMON:
Norbert drives me,
Veronica feeds us,   NORBERT:
Yolanda sings, Peter   I fix things.
plays, Father holds us
all together. God gives
everybody a job, and I
make sure things are
okay. I watch. I watch   LOTTIE:
the building. I watch   And what do I do, nothing?
the cars. All night. I'm a
twenty-four hour security
system. It's what I'm
meant to do. And I have
to be paid for that! It's
only fair. And I don't
need much. And I give
a lot back. Remember
that time I scared away
the burglar—just by
turning on a light? Last
week I saw a fire in the
education building, cause
I was here. Nobody else
was here at four in the
morning—that's what *I* do.
So I'm the one who got the
fire extinguisher—

VERONICA: Except there was no fire.

SIMON: And I'm sorry about that.

VERONICA:
You spray the fire
extinguisher all over
everything—

NORBERT:
Hoo-boy! What a mess!

SIMON: But I cleaned it up! I do that, too! I have to have
something to do or I go, well, you know how I go—

PASTOR: You have a lot of energy—

SIMON: I get depressed, and when I do, you know, I,
sometimes, in the past—

PASTOR: But not recently—

SIMON:
Not just pills, but sharp
things—

NORBERT:
We're glad you're here to
help, Simon.

SIMON: You tried to get me in that program, Father,
but I just couldn't—I'm not homeless, this is my home!
This is what I need, the church is what I need! But I
have to get paid!

PASTOR: *(Giving him money)* Here.

VERONICA & NORBERT:
(Disappointed)
Pastor.

GUSTAFINA:
Pastor, we are going soon,
ja?

SIMON:
Otherwise, you'll be
having my funeral here.
Father, I can have my
funeral here, can't I?

PASTOR:
In just a few minutes,
Gustafina.

PASTOR: That's a long ways off, Simon.

LOTTIE: And I can sing at it.

(They all look at LOTTIE.*)*

LOTTIE: I've decided to become a funeral singer. Full
time. So I might be retiring as office manager soon. I

know a lot of sad songs, in a variety of faith traditions. Let everybody know.

SIMON: Thanks, Father.

PASTOR: Simon, I'm not a priest—I'm a minister. A pastor, not a father.

SIMON: You're a father to me. *(Looking at money)* Anyone wanna go to Jack-in-the-Box? My treat?

LARRY: No thanks.

NORBERT: If you can wait, Simon, I'll give you a ride.

SIMON: I'm okay. It's not far. Good night. *(Runs out)*

NORBERT: Pastor, we don't have that kind of money—

VERONICA: You're just encouraging him—

PASTOR: Think of it as an informal homeless ministry— we can't afford a real program—whatsoever you do unto the least of these, you do unto me—

NORBERT:	PASTOR:
We're in a financial crisis. If I don't find another renter to replace the school—	The church is sposed to be a refuge from the world—

PASTOR: It's *my* money, Norbert. Not the church's.

NORBERT:	GUSTAFINA:
But still—	What time is it?

LARRY: If we had an endowment, we could have a *formal* homeless ministry.

PASTOR: Time for me to take you home. Norbert, don't panic—pray. *A bientôt*, everyone.

EVERYONE: *(Variously)* Good night, *au revoir*, Pastor. Good night, *guten nacht*, Gustafina.

GUSTAFINA: Good night.

(PASTOR and GUSTAFINA leave.)

VERONICA:
Oh, Lottie, I found a
typo—

LOTTIE:
I thought you proofed it
already.

VERONICA:
Sorry. I'll fix it. Don't
worry about it—

NORBERT:
Larry, I don't know if you
know I've decided being
president of the
congregation is just a little
too much for me,
overwhelming, you
know—

LARRY:
You're really good at it,
Norbert. I can see that from
just my one year on
Council—

LOTTIE: No, it's my job. *(Takes papers and leaves)*

NORBERT: Well, heh, heh, thanks very much, Larry. But
I was thinking it's time for me to take a break—I've
been president for the last eight years—

VERONICA: And you did such a good job leading the
organ campaign before that— *(Disappears)*

NORBERT: But I was talking to Veronica—

LARRY: Wait, no, I think I know where this is going—

NORBERT: I'm getting older, not moving as fast,
and I get this nervous rash—I'm just not very
confrontational, and I'm getting a little tired—

LARRY: Are you saying I'm confrontational—?

NORBERT: No, but you have a lot of ideas—

LARRY: And the tradition around here seems to be if
you have an idea—

NORBERT: Then you get asked to carry it out, that's
right—I know how you feel. Sometimes life just seems
like a series of getting through things—if I can only
get through *this week*, if I can only finish *that*. And it's a
little hard to see what's on the other side—what's there

after all the hard work? What's the reward? Are you just trying to *get through* your whole life—?

LARRY: You're sure an upbeat mix of the eighties, nineties, and today—

NORBERT: A kind of mild agony all the time—

LARRY: Are you asking me—what are you asking me?

NORBERT: Just to think about—I know you've only been on Council a year, but the website project turned out great—

LARRY: You want me to be president?

NORBERT: Well, I suppose…would you think about it?

LARRY: But I'm just barely a Lutheran. I only started coming to church when you decided to pay Yolanda for choir, what, a year and a half ago?

NORBERT: But then you joined choir, joined Council, got baptized—

(VERONICA *comes out, starts tidying up the choir area.*)

LARRY: Six months ago! I don't know anything about it. I only started taking communion last month.

NORBERT: See? How fast you move? That's what we need. Lutherans tend to be too cautious—it's our nature, heh, heh.

LARRY: Look, I love this place. Everybody talks too much, but in my family *nobody* talked, so all this chatter's kinda fun—

VERONICA: I think you'd be a great president. Attendance would soar!

LARRY: Veronica, I'm not ready for that—I've got too many jobs—overbooked as it is—

VERONICA:	NORBERT:
Oh, I completely understand—	It *is* a big commitment—

VERONICA: Everybody here is doing so much—

NORBERT: The nature of a small church—you're doing *way* too much, Veronica—

VERONICA:	LARRY:
(Lifting a stack of music folders) Oh, no, I do as much as I want to—	Always here. Quietly taking care of things.

LARRY: *(Helping her)* Why don't you be president?

VERONICA: It's really not my place— *(Dropping the folders)* Oops—sorry—I didn't drop any on you, did I? *(Going to her knees to pick them up.)*

LARRY: *(Kneeling to help)* No, I'm fine—here—

NORBERT: *(Also kneeling and gathering folders)* I'll get some—you shouldn't be lifting that much anyways.

VERONICA: *(Standing, with some folders in her arms)* Oh, no, I'm fine. *(As she stands, she accidentally catches her wig on a chair or pew, and it comes off. She is completely bald.)*

LARRY:	NORBERT:
Veronica—	Your wig—

VERONICA: Oh, dear. *(Putting the wig back on)* I'm just not used to this thing. It keeps slipping off.

LARRY: What—are you—?

VERONICA: Chemotherapy. You knew that, didn't you?

LARRY:	NORBERT:
Well, no, Peter mentioned—I'm sorry. What kind—?	That's why we've been praying for her every week—

VERONICA: I had a mastectomy two months ago.

LARRY: But…when? You didn't miss church.

NORBERT: She came to choir four days after the operation. Hoo-boy.

VERONICA: I couldn't just sit home. But don't worry. I'm fine. I take the wig off at the community center when I want to scare the kids.

LARRY: Don't you think you're doing too much—if you're not up to snuff?

VERONICA: I feel fine. I vomit a lot the day after my treatment, then I'm okay. Or pretty much.

NORBERT: But this is why she shouldn't be president.

LARRY:	VERONICA:
I didn't know. I thought some kind of stomach thing—	It's no big deal. But you'd make a wonderful president, Larry.

NORBERT: Wonderful.

VERONICA: If you do it, I'd be willing to be vice president and do all the annoying stuff.

LARRY: But—

VERONICA: Oh, I understand if you don't have the time—

LARRY: It's not that—

VERONICA: We're all so busy.

NORBERT: But we need some fresh thinking—

VERONICA: Business savvy—

NORBERT:	
We're in a little bit of a crisis with the school leaving at the end of the month—	VERONICA: The savings are pretty depleted.

LARRY: But you gotta know that if I'm president I'm gonna want to deal with that my way. No more council meetings where everybody talks and nothing happens.

(PASTOR *comes in with a toilet plunger.*)

NORBERT:	VERONICA:
That's why we want you.	Of course. That's what
A bold approach. Lots of	we're hoping for.
energy!	An answer to a prayer.

LARRY: That's the problem! We can't pray ourselves out of this mess!

PASTOR: God has an answer for every prayer. But not always the one you expect. What mess? *(He gives each of them an odd look in turn, then disappears into the sacristy.)*

LARRY: Okay, okay, I'll think about it.

NORBERT: You will?

VERONICA: Oh, Larry, that's wonderful. *(Hugs him)* I'm so happy.

YOLANDA: *(Having finished her song)* What's wonderful?

LARRY: I…uh…I'll tell you in the car.

YOLANDA: Wonderful would be if people would actually listen while someone's trying to practice, rather than jabber on about nothing, dumping folders—

LARRY:	VERONICA:
Home again, home again,	I'm sorry, Yolanda.
jiggity jig.	

YOLANDA: Finally and at last! Thank you, Peter.

PETER: You're welcome. It sounded great.

VERONICA: Beautiful, Yolanda.

YOLANDA: Thanks, Veronica.

(As he and YOLANDA leave:)

LARRY: I want you to know I'm really flattered—but—

NORBERT: Just think about it.

LARRY: And Veronica, I'm sorry about—

VERONICA: It's nothing. I'm fine. Good night.

YOLANDA: LARRY:
Why are you flattered?   Get a good night's sleep,
Peter.

LARRY: PETER:
In the car.   I'll count sermons.

YOLANDA: I have a right to know—

LARRY: Can you for once not think about something so trivial—!

YOLANDA: Trivial!

(YOLANDA *and* LARRY *leave.*)

NORBERT: I'll take care of the lights. *(He starts turning out the lights.)*

PETER: They sure bicker a lot.

VERONICA: Oh, she's just jealous.

PETER: Jealous!?

VERONICA: She's irritated he flirts with you.

PETER: He does not! He teases—

VERONICA: He teases everybody—so funny. But he flirts with you, *Petey.*

PETER: Veronica, that's embarrassing. And not true.

VERONICA: Well, I'm sure you read that kind of thing better than I do. But you're talented and interesting—

PETER: I am *not* interesting!

VERONICA: Everybody is, if you look close enough.

PETER: But there's never any time for that. I'm not going to read anything more into Larry. Besides it's irrelevant. He's got a girlfriend and I—

VERONICA: You have your music.

PETER: Mean!

VERONICA: You're above love.

PETER: Make fun.

VERONICA: You said it before: "I'm above love."

PETER: No, I said I'm over it. Love is hormonal. We've romanticized it, but now that I'm older I realize it's just biology. It used to feel so *insistent*, but now I could give a—I could care less. Besides, my mother's coming to live with me. And you're right. I have a lot of things to do. There's the hospital, there's church, and I have a feeling I'm going to compose something really amazing someday. Music that makes a difference, brings people back to church. That organ cantata—I'm not too old for that, although they say composition is for young people, too.

VERONICA: Mozart was composing at four and burnt out by—

PETER: He was dead before he was my age. But people live longer now.

VERONICA: Some people.

PETER: Stop that! Veronica!

(VERONICA *laughs.*)

PETER: That's not funny. You're so bratty. You paid for the altar flowers again this month, didn't you?

VERONICA: The ladies pay for the flowers—in memory of their husbands—

PETER: What do you care about all those old f— (*Catches himself*) —Fellows under the altar?

VERONICA: They do! The widows. They pay!

PETER: Whatever you say. But you do too much! You're always here, and you never get anything back!

VERONICA:
Oh, I get plenty back,
all the time. Just to be   PETER:

around Pastor. I admire him so much. He's so quietly spiritual, which stands out in our loud world.

And that shameless manipulation to get Larry to be president—

VERONICA: Norbert asked Larry to be president.

PETER: But—your wig—how could he say no?

VERONICA: That was a complete accident. I should probably glue it to my head.

NORBERT: *(Calling out)* Everybody out. I'm turning out the lights.

PETER: I saw. It was not an accident.

VERONICA: Yes, it was!

PETER:
I can just imagine you cooking that up with Pastor over the dishes. Hey, did you smell wine on his breath tonight, by the way? What was that—late afternoon communion?

VERONICA:
If I were that cagey, the church wouldn't be having financial problems—don't be so hard on him. He's got a lot on his mind.

PETER: And are you so sure Larry would make a good president? Some of his ideas are a little aggressive, hard-edged, *practical*.

PETER:
I'm not sure I trust him. Scares me a bit.

VERONICA:
He's so good with money.

VERONICA: Don't *trust* him?

PETER: Orange Grove is at a delicate point, and Larry— well, he's not the delicate type—

VERONICA: You're just saying that because he flirts with you.

(Sees PASTOR coming in with the plunger. His shirt is wet.)

VERONICA: Pastor!

PETER: Weren't you taking Gustafina home?

NORBERT: Lights out!

PASTOR: Did the wig trick work?

(Blackout as NORBERT shuts off all the lights.)

END OF ACT ONE

ACT TWO

(VERONICA *comes in and turns off the house lights and adjusts the others.* PASTOR *comes in, followed by* PETER. *When she finishes with the lights, she putters about, tidying up the choir area.*)

PETER: It just hardly seems worth it this year, and maybe too painful for everybody.

PASTOR: We always start Lent with the distribution of ashes—nothing's changed—

PETER: Not yet. But I don't want to go out into the night with our future smudged on my forehead. If Larry has his way—you're not happy about—tonight—I mean, it's *practical*, but—

PASTOR: We'll see how things work out.

PETER: But it's not like you don't have a say! You're letting this place slip through your fingers—in the last year attendance fell from fifty to thirty-some at a service—

PASTOR: Peter, I know you're anxious, but a church is based on faith—

PETER: I'm not anxious—sad is all.

PASTOR: We're not the only church in this position. Mount Olive's the same. All across the country Lutheran churches—plenty of mainline Protestant churches—have attendance of thirty, twenty, even less than ten at a service, and they keep going—

PETER: Wherever two or three are gathered—

PASTOR:	PETER:
The numbers don't matter so much. Miracles are small things, happening one at a time, to a few people here and there.	They're dying! But in life aren't we supposed to be headed toward something, pushing toward a goal, moving—

PASTOR: Well, certainly. There's one thing we're all moving toward all the time. No matter how much we accomplish—

VERONICA: Death.

PETER: Veronica! *(Laughs)* Scared me! Popped up like a ghost.

(VERONICA wails like a ghost.)

PASTOR: I was thinking *after* death. But we do have to get through the death part first.

PETER: Is that what's happening here? I don't see how I'm gonna get through tonight.

VERONICA: Concentrate on Yolanda breaking up with Larry.

PETER: Veronica!

VERONICA: Oh, that's right. Pastor, Peter's above love.

PETER: They're not breaking up. They just think it's healthier not to live together right now.

VERONICA: You'd think they'd come to *Pastor* for counseling.

PASTOR: Are they *both* telling you what's wrong with the other?

PETER:	PASTOR:
No! A little. Larry more	They should at least get

than Yolanda.   advice from someone
                                 slightly neutral!

VERONICA: You're not above love at all.

PETER: Both of you! Stop it! You're being catty cause
you're afraid—this isn't pretty, it isn't! When really it's
as much your fault as anybody's—you're supposed to
be in charge of the budget—

VERONICA: Perhaps we shouldn't have let you hire all
those musicians for Good Friday and Easter, when
there's no way we can afford them—

PASTOR: Oh, we have to have the tympani—

PETER: Fine!

PASTOR: And the brass—

VERONICA: PASTOR:
You threatened to quit if   And the oboe!
we didn't—

PETER: Make fun! At least I act like it's serious! We can
say "oh, this isn't important, this too shall pass,"—
something's got to be important *sometime*!

VERONICA: PASTOR:
Peter, you're overreacting!   Of course, it's serious.

PETER: I am *not* overreacting!

(PETER *runs out and there's the sound of him tripping over
something and falling down, perhaps triggering a car alarm.)*

(As VERONICA *and* PASTOR *rush to the door and look out:)*

VERONICA: Peter!

PASTOR: *(Trying not to giggle)* Are you okay?

PETER: *(Off)* Peachy! I just—go abuse Simon!

PASTOR: He's limping.   .

VERONICA: He just tripped over the curb.

PASTOR: Should we be worried about him?

(Coming in, assisting GUSTAFINA:*)*

LOTTIE: Almost knocked Mrs Liedtke down.

GUSTAFINA: I hope Peter's all right. *(Giggles)* But he did look funny.

PASTOR: His ego's bruised more than anything.

VERONICA: Gustafina, are you feeling all right?

GUSTAFINA: Just a little dizzy in the parking lot. I'll be fine.

LOTTIE: *(Holding up some small metal rings.)* Mrs Liedtke, can you pull these apart?

GUSTAFINA: Oh, don't ask me!

LOTTIE: Pastor?

PASTOR: *(Trying)* No, they're linked together. They were forged that way.

LOTTIE: *(Pulling the rings apart) Voila!*

VERONICA:	PASTOR:
Oh my!	Lottie, most excellent!

VERONICA:	LOTTIE:
You take our minds off— keep us distracted—	I gotta have some kinda alternative career.

PASTOR: *(Overlapping)* If Peter'd come back maybe we could rehearse.

YOLANDA:	VERONICA:
(Coming in) Where's Peter going? I thought I was gonna be late.	Oh, good, Yolanda. Are you going to be here Shrove Sunday? I need some help making my famous layer loaf.

YOLANDA: *(Rolling her eyes)* Sorry. I'm rehearsing for my master class. Pastor, when you go to Paris next time, can I come with you?

PASTOR:
Won't you and Larry
want to be in Paris
alone? I'd most certainly
be in your way.

YOLANDA:
No, I'll want your
advice—where to eat,
what to see—not just
touristy stuff—

PASTOR:
(*Showing her a letter*)
Speaking of Paris, I just
got this letter from Taizé,
sent to Mount Olive by
mistake—isn't that funny?
They're inviting me to
stay again next time I'm
in France. Longer even—

GUSTAFINA:
Why Paris? Why not
Weimar? It is the soul of
Germany. Goethehaus,
Schillerhaus, Liszthaus,
all the literature and music.
Such music they play there.
A beautiful place—*schön*!

LOTTIE:
Right next to Buchenwald,
isn't it?

GUSTAFINA: Longer than vacation?

PASTOR: Oranges and olives don't taste very good
together, you know.

GUSTAFINA & YOLANDA: What?

PASTOR: I made an olive-orange relish the other day
to go with my Cornish game hen, but it was terrible.
Maybe it was the pomegranate juice.

YOLANDA: Ew! You didn't!

VERONICA: Never mind. Pastor, please! Yolanda, I
didn't know you and Larry were planning to go to
Paris.

YOLANDA: We're not. *(Announcing to everyone)* Oh, Larry's probably going to be very late. He's off at Mount Olive—

VERONICA: With Norbert. We know.

YOLANDA: Just passing it on. He asked me to.

PASTOR: Norbert's got that commitment from the Schermers—

VERONICA: The alternate plan—

GUSTAFINA: How much is the amount, Pastor?

PASTOR: Five thousand dollars. In writing.

GUSTAFINA:	LOTTIE:	YOLANDA:
Oh.	Not enough…	That won't do it.

VERONICA: It's a start. Sort of a challenge grant for the other thirty-five—

PETER: *(Coming in, very business-like)* Lottie, we need to start even though not everyone's here. Can you and Steve get us into Gethsemane?

LOTTIE:	YOLANDA:
(Putting her recorder together) Sure.	Steve?

	PASTOR:
PETER:	Her recorder.
Pastor, the tenor part is really important in this, and Simon's not here yet—	YOLANDA: Oh, right, Steve.

PASTOR: So you want me to sing a solo?

PETER: Until Simon arrives it'll be a solo.

PASTOR: I shall be pleased to uphold tenor honor.

PETER: Veronica, we'll need you back in the soprano section as well. May I count on you?

VERONICA: Most assuredly. *(Giggles)*

PETER: Norbert and Larry will be here late or maybe even not at all. Larry's taking his proposal, the one approved by church council—

VERONICA: Tentatively—

PETER: What?

VERONICA:	YOLANDA:
Tentatively approved. Conditional upon acceptance by Mount Olive.	Larry's saying it's a done deal.

PASTOR: Peter, shouldn't we begin?

PETER: Of course, I just thought everyone should know—

VERONICA: Everyone knows.

PETER: Oh. Okay. Lottie? Steve?

(LOTTIE plays a verse of Go To Dark Gethsemane on her recorder. She's not particularly good. Everyone else scrambles for their music and gets ready to sing. GUSTAFINA holds her head for a moment. VERONICA notices and puts her hand on GUSTAFINA'S shoulder, but GUSTAFINA shakes it off impatiently. They begin to sing. Missing SIMON, LARRY and NORBERT, they don't sound very good, either.)

EVERYONE: *(In parts)*
Go to dark Gethsemane
All who feel the tempter's pow'r.
Your Redeemer's conflict see.
Watch with him one bitter hour
Turn not from his griefs away;
Learn from Jesus Christ to pray.

SIMON: *(Bursting in)* The church is sold!

GUSTAFINA: PASTOR:
What? No!   Simon!
(Starts to cry)

VERONICA: LOTTIE:
Simon, stop that! It's not   It couldn't be sold that fast!
true. Larry and Norbert
just went to Mount
Olive's council—

SIMON: It's sold!

PASTOR: YOLANDA:
Simon, what makes you   Did Larry tell you?
say that? How do you
know?

SIMON: No.

PETER: LOTTIE:
Simon, sit down please.   Sit down!

VERONICA: Norbert?

SIMON: No.

PETER: Your presence is formally requested in the tenor
section.

VERONICA: Then who, Simon?

LOTTIE: You're just making it up. You're like a dog that
pees on the carpet just to get attention. I used to believe
you, feel sorry for you, but you *always* exaggerate—you
always need money for something—

PASTOR: Lottie—

LOTTIE: YOLANDA:
I know. Out of bounds!   Now who's trying to get
I'm too forthright, too   attention?
honest, never sparing
anyone's feelings—

PASTOR: No one says that about you, Lottie.

LOTTIE: But what about my feelings? You can all just go to Mount Olive—but this is my job!

YOLANDA: A goofy one.

PASTOR:	YOLANDA:
Yolanda!	So easy!

LOTTIE: It just looks easy because I've got the office organized.

LOTTIE:	VERONICA:
It's part time and it	Well, sort of.
doesn't pay much,	
but it's perfect—	
perfect for me, anyway.	
I've worked at a lot of	
places—but nowhere	YOLANDA:
was everybody—	I bet she has.
most everybody—	
so nice!	

VERONICA: It's not confirmed, Lottie.

SIMON: It is!

PASTOR:	LOTTIE:
Who told you, Simon?	I'm consulting an attorney.

SIMON: I just *know*. Sometimes I know things. Is it okay if I know something? (*Bumping into* VERONICA'*s coffee cup, spilling it*) Oh, sorry.

VERONICA:	SIMON:
My coffee! Simon!	You believe me, don't you, Yolanda?

PETER:	LOTTIE:
Simon, sit down and take	Please just be quiet!
your Ritalin!	

PASTOR:	YOLANDA:	SIMON:
It's a *feeling*—	I won't believe it	What's Ritalin?

is that right?   till I hear it from   I don't take
                        Larry.   Ritalin!

SIMON: Yeah. I'll clean it up.

VERONICA: *(Relaxing as she cleans)* No, no, I shouldn't have coffee in here.

LOTTIE: No, you shouldn't.

VERONICA: Just a feeling.

GUSTAFINA: SIMON:
Sehr gut. I have been here   But it's strong!
since I was twenty-two!

PASTOR: VERONICA:
Simon, we're not thinking   *(Tasting the coffee*
about that now. We're   *remnant)*
singing. And I, for one,   It's *weak*, if anything.
feel the need of another
tenor.

SIMON: GUSTAFINA:
Okay. Sure. What song?   *(Holding her head again)*
(PASTOR *shows him.)*   I don't know if I'm up to all
                                    this.

YOLANDA: SIMON:
(To LOTTIE)   Don't be scared, Pastor.
Maybe it's retirement time.
                                    PASTOR:
LOTTIE: I'm not scared.
Shhh!
                                    SIMON:
                                    Your music's shaking.
                                    Don't panic—pray.

(After they all stare at PETER *expectantly.)*

PETER: Oh. Is it time to rehearse? Could there possibly be a *church service* on Sunday?

PASTOR: As far as we know.

PETER: Maybe even with *music*?

VERONICA: I'm sorry, Peter. I'll behave, won't I, Gustafina?

GUSTAFINA: Ja, sure.

PETER: Okay, if we're actually *ready*—we need to break this down a bit. And since we're short of men—

SIMON: Hey!

PASTOR: We have the requisite number of tenors, thank you.

PETER: *(Exasperated)* Yes, Father.

SIMON: *(Correcting)* Pastor!

PETER: *(Glaring at* SIMON*)* —Let's have just the women on verse two.

(Singing in parts, as PETER *plays:)*

WOMEN:
Follow to the judgment hall
View the Lord of Life arraigned—

YOLANDA: *(Interrupting)* Before we do that, I think I have to tell everyone that Larry and I are no longer— we're not—

LOTTIE:	VERNONICA:
Together?	*(With a glance at* PETER*)*
	An item?

YOLANDA:	SIMON:
We're not—I don't want	You broke up?
to talk about it, but, well,	
we're *not*. I just thought	
you should know so there	
won't be any question.	PASTOR: Shhh, Simon,
	please.

PETER: *(After a moment of silence)* I'm sorry,
Yolanda. Thank you. We're all appreciative of your
thoughtfulness about our feelings.

YOLANDA: I just don't want there to be any question.

PETER: No. Of course not. Not one. We're very sorry to
hear it.

*(Ad lib agreement: "Yes. Of course, very sorry. That's
terrible.")*

SIMON: *(Not meaning a word of it)* That's awful. Just
awful!

GUSTAFINA: May I just say one thing?

(Everyone tenses.)

PETER: Yes, Gustafina?

GUSTAFINA: I have been hearing from the ladies that
they're a little—nothing against anyone here, but, well,
they miss the Tre Ore service.

LOTTIE: Not again.

PETER: We had a vote on that in Council, I thought—	*(SIMON gets up and moves next to YOLANDA, which makes her uncomfortable.)*

PASTOR: We did. Gustafina, perhaps—

GUSTAFINA: *(Overlapping)* I'm only saying that I've
heard—it's hard for them to come to Tenebrae at night
on Good Friday, and they miss the afternoon service,
that's all—

PETER: Which ladies, Gustafina?

GUSTAFINA	LOTTIE
Oh, they wouldn't want me to say.	I know who it is.

PETER: I wish they'd said something when we were
deciding. It's a little late now.

GUSTAFINA: Oh, they would never say. But I thought I should pass on—

PASTOR:
Thank you, Gustafina.

PETER:
That's very helpful. Simon, back to the tenor section!

VERONICA: For next year.

(SIMON *returns to his place with some reluctance.*)

LOTTIE: If there is a next year.

PETER: Verse two? Without Steve this time. Ladies only?

YOLANDA:
(*Mimicking* PETER*)*
Ladies only?

SIMON:
Father, I mean, Pastor, you think I'm wrong about the church being sold, but I can hear it in my head.

PETER:
Please?
(*Plays*)

PASTOR:
I'm sure that's true, Simon.

WOMEN:
(*Singing in parts*)
Follow to the judgment hall,
View the Lord of Life arraigned;
Oh, the wormwood and the gall!
Oh, the pangs his soul sustained!
Shun not suff'ring, shame, or loss;
Learn from him to bear the cross.

SIMON:
You're just saying that. You don't believe me. No one ever believes me. (*Louder*) It's my great misfortune never to be believed. Nobody takes me seriously because of my face. I don't have a serious face. It's a kind of

PETER: comical face.
Simon, let's be polite and
listen when the others are
singing.

SIMON: See, no one takes me seriously! I'm a serious
guy. The church is sold and I don't have anywhere else
to go and I'm serious!

PETER: Simon, please! Were you raised by—manatees?!

YOLANDA: (Mimicking PETER) Simon, please!

LOTTIE: SIMON:
Yolanda, what is your   I can't be polite if no one
deal?   takes me seriously!

PETER: Simon, we take you seriously enough to let
you live on church property for free which is probably
completely illegal, and it's only happening because
Pastor's too soft-hearted to kick you out and made up
a whole "watchman" job for you so you can feel you're
contributing when in actuality you're just a kind of
parasite who's found a good host—!

PASTOR: VERONICA:
Peter—   Simon, you're getting all
                                      sweaty.

PETER: SIMON:
I'm just sick of you   You're not paying me!
 interrupting and   If that's how taking all of
this generosity—   you feel, I might as well
killing the fatted   quit.
calf—for granted—

VERONICA: (Giving SIMON a cloth) Here, wipe your face.

(SIMON does.)

YOLANDA: Simon, please. We're all very glad you're
here and your voice is beautiful.

SIMON: It is?

YOLANDA: When you listen to Peter and sing like he says.

PETER:	SIMON:
But how often does *that* happen?!	Okay, Yolanda, I won't quit.
PASTOR:	VERONICA:
Peter—	This is a rough night for all of us—

PETER: I'm sorry, Pastor, but I'm sick, sick, sick of all— this—verse three, please—everybody! *(Plays)*

EVERYONE: *(In harmony, sounding somewhat better, but lacking basses)*
Calv'ry's mournful mountain climb;
There, adoring at his feet,

(NORBERT arrives, looking very distracted. Everyone glances at him, but the singing continues uninterrupted.)

EVERYONE:
Mark that miracle of time,
God's own sacrifice complete.

(SIMON starts fanning for personal gas again. PETER notices and picks up a hymnal.)

EVERYONE:
"It is finished!" hear him cry;
Learn from Jesus Christ to die.

(At the conclusion of the song, PETER throws the hymnal at SIMON.)

PETER: Simon, stop it!

(But the hymnal hits LARRY, who has just come in the room.)

LARRY: Hey! Ow!

PETER: Sorry, Larry, that was meant for Simon. Simon! No more! I won't have it!

LARRY: Won't have what?

VERONICA: SIMON:
Simon, would you like   Yolanda, you can smell it,
some lemonade?   can't you?
Let's go get some—

PETER: Veronica, no! We need to be responsible—

VERONICA: PETER:
Our responsibility is to   Simon needs to know when
help each other without   he's out of—
asking questions. That's
what we do. When you
needed a full-time job,
Pastor got you in at the
hospital—

PASTOR: You did that, Veronica—

VERONICA: Well, whatever, it was *done*. Nothing else
matters very much, does it? We try to be nice, try to be
polite—it doesn't always work, but we try. And that's
what counts, right, Peter?

PETER: I guess.

(They all look at PETER.*)*

PETER: I'm sorry, Simon.

SIMON: Me, too.

PETER: *(After a moment)* Norbert?

NORBERT: Oh. Hello. Sorry we're late.

LARRY: *(Bursting with news)* Yeah, we didn't mean to
interrupt—

NORBERT: I drove kinda slowly cause my blood
pressure's been bothering me—I've got the blood
pressure of a small rodent, must be part gopher, heh-
heh, my heartbeat's abnormally fast, too—and I've
been feeling kinda funny, plus traffic was terrible,

keeps getting worse and worse on Santa Monica
Boulevard—

PASTOR: The whole West Side—

NORBERT: Hoo—yeah! Just terrible, worse every year—
and the airplanes from Santa Monica airport fly over
my house—

LARRY: *(Bursting out impatiently)* They accepted our
proposal!

(Everyone just stares at LARRY.)

LARRY: Mount Olive was very enthusiastic about
merging congregations. Their attendance is almost
as bad as ours, so this is an opportunity to double—
they've got plenty of room in the pews! And it's a
very nice facility—not as much character as Orange
Grove Lutheran, but much more modern, better
parking, no building maintenance problems. And with
a real endowment they—*we*—can makes substantial
improvements and develop new programs—they're
even open to the idea of moving our organ into their
sanctuary—

PETER:	LOTTIE:
You can't—move—	Do they need an office
an organ—	manager?

NORBERT:	LARRY:	SIMON:
I told him that.	What?	I was right.
		Believe me now?

VERONICA: The pipes—

PETER: The console, the whole design—it's for this
sanctuary—almost impossible to adapt. It'll never
sound the same—

YOLANDA:	PETER:
The acoustics—	It was built to my

	specifications—*our* specifications—just for us!
GUSTAFINA: So the church—?	PETER: Look—the pipes— how beautiful! It just fits! Maybe it's idolatrous,
SIMON: Is sold!	but I *love* this organ!

VERONICA: The church isn't sold. They've accepted our proposal, that's all. We have the option—

LARRY: They accepted our proposal and don't forget I've been talking to a developer and today he made an offer of one point seven million—one point seven million!—imagine what good we can do with that—

| PETER:
—At Mount Olive— | GUSTAFINA:
So the church—? |

LARRY: (*Enthusiastically*) It's as good as sold!

(VERONICA *throws down her keys and storms out.* PETER *disappears.*)

LARRY: Of course it's a sad day, but it's a happy one as well—a new beginning. You made me president cause you thought I had ideas, could get things done—and the Council agreed to my proposal. We don't have much choice—but this is a good thing! We've saved the church—not its sanctuary, but its soul! You'll see. Right, Pastor?

(PASTOR *does not answer.* PETER *reappears with a number of small, white boxes. He stacks them up in a prominent place as* LARRY *is talking, then disappears again.*)

LARRY: And here's the really cool part! I had no idea why my father was so attached to this place, why he wanted to garden here when there were lots better jobs all around town. In investigating the title I found

out who owned this property before it belonged to the
church. It's amazing! Can you guess?

(No one guesses. PETER *returns with more small white
boxes and continues stacking them. When he finishes, he
disappears.)*

LARRY: My grandfather! My grandfather owned this
land before the war. It was his orange grove—those
were his trees! He lost it during the internment,
apparently he had to sell the land cheap— *(To*
GUSTAFINA*)* So I guess you got a good deal! Isn't that
astonishing? I'm flabbergasted myself. My father never
told me, just worked and worked what was left of the
land after he got out of the camp. Till there were no
more trees—except the one. He loved to bring me here,
let me fertilize—

LARRY:	GUSTAFINA:
Did you know about that?	You were always so dirty!
Did you know you got	
my grandfather's land?	

(It seems GUSTAFINA *can't answer.* PETER *returns with
more white boxes, stacking them.)*

YOLANDA:	LOTTIE:
Larry, shut up!	Peter, what are you doing?

PASTOR: Yolanda, kindly—

YOLANDA: You are so clueless! This is why we broke-
up—

*(*LARRY *starts to react.)*

YOLANDA: —Yes, I told them! I can think for myself
now. You just put on your big old boots and stomp all
over everybody. And you don't even know! No idea of
the effect you have. You're a klutz.

LARRY: Yolanda—

YOLANDA: *(Surprisingly vehement)* Klutz!

SIMON: You're right, Yolanda, he's a klutz! *(To* LARRY*)* Klutz!

YOLANDA: I sang my first solo here! *(She starts to cry.)*

LOTTIE: Peter, are those—?

PETER: The church fathers. Fred Briscoe, George Morgenthaler, Arky Hannu, Harvey Johnson—

*(*VERONICA *enters and gathers her things.)*

LARRY:	SIMON:	NORBERT:
Peter, that's disrespectful.	Ew! That's weird!	Arky helped me build the baptismal font.

PETER:	LOTTIE:
Here's Pastor Liedtke!	Pastor, stop him!

YOLANDA:	NORBERT
Peter, don't be disgusting! Gustafina, he's sorry—	George was pretty handy, too.

PETER:	VERONICA:
Not at all! They're bearing witness.	They remind us of the past, and we're showing them the future—

PETER: —Or lack thereof!

VERONICA:	PETER:
Where will we put them? Does Mount Olive have a columbarium?	There won't be an altar for them to hide under any more. Their wives won't take them back—

PASTOR:	SIMON:
Peter, Peter, please. *(Trying not to cry)* Do not—do not make light—	He's freaking me out, Pastor. I might go over the edge. Dead! Whole people! In little boxes!

PETER: I'm not—just pointing out the—I dunno—
irony—that's probably not the right word—

PASTOR: I think what we have to think of here, if I'm
not mistaken, is to remember the Bible. There is no
shame in this.

LARRY: Shame?

PASTOR: No shame. There is glory. You don't always
have to win. We don't always have to have the most
members, or the most people in church on a Sunday—
the numbers don't mean much. Sometimes you win by
losing.

VERONICA: You must lose your life to save it.

LARRY: Mrs. Liedtke, did you know? Did your husband
tell you how the church bought the land? Who sold it?

(GUSTAFINA *appears to be trying to talk, but can't seem to
get the words out.*)

PETER:	YOLANDA:
Larry, you're	Stop bugging her. She's
embarrassing her.	old!

LARRY: It's just a simple—

GUSTAFINA: I—I—I— (*Gestures helplessly, looks
imploringly at* VERONICA.)

YOLANDA: Really old.

LARRY: I'm sorry, Mrs Liedtke—I didn't mean—

PASTOR: (*Going to her*) Gustafina, are you all right?

GUSTAFINA: (*Looking frightened and helpless, a hand to her
head*) I—I—I—

LOTTIE:	PASTOR:
Is she—?	Veronica, what do you
	think?

NORBERT:
Oh, my, I think she's
having a stroke—

VERONICA:
Gustafina, can you raise
your arms?

YOLANDA:
(*To* LARRY)
Look what you did!

SIMON:
I can help! What can I do?

VERONICA:
Can you say anything?

LARRY:
I didn't—

YOLANDA:
Klutz!

LARRY:
It's just the truth,
that's all.

GUSTAFINA:
I—I—

VERONICA:
Anything else?

LARRY:
It was Petey with the
ashes—

GUSTAFINA:
I—

PETER:
Don't call me
Petey!

YOLANDA:
Put a pencil
between her teeth!

VERONICA:
I think it is a stroke.
Lottie, call an ambulance.

PASTOR:
No, that's for a seizure.

(LOTTIE *jumps up and runs out.*)

PETER:
I'm parked right outside.

YOLANDA:
She could choke on her
tongue!

VERONICA:
Go start your car.

SIMON:
What can I do? Let me
help!

(PETER *runs out.*)

NORBERT:
Those look like the
symptoms. I read about
this because I have high
blood pressure, too.

PASTOR:
Gustafina, give me your
hand.

VERONICA: YOLANDA:
Larry, help us help her   Larry, help, for heaven's
out. Gustafina, can you   sake!
walk? Let's walk.

(They help GUSTAFINA *walk toward the door.)*

(It's a struggle. NORBERT *fades the lights while* YOLANDA
stands by in judgment and SIMON *hovers uselessly.)*

VERONICA: PASTOR: SIMON:
Careful, careful, One step at a   Let me! Let me!
you're doing   time.
great—

YOLANDA: NORBERT
They didn't mean it,   This is why they have
Gustafina—   A D A requirements.

VERONICA: PASTOR: SIMON:
Almost there—   Most excellent— I'm watching!

LARRY: NORBERT: YOLANDA:
I didn't think— We'll all be old, Klutz!
                 soon.

VERONICA: PASTOR: SIMON:
Peter's bringing Just relax.   Do you just want
his car.   me to watch?

LARRY: YOLANDA:
I'm so sorry, Mrs Liedtke,   Larry's sorry, Gustafina.
I didn't know— I just got   Peter's sorry, too, I'm
so excited—this is a   sure—
wonderful day for me!
For all of us! A wonderful
day!

*(Lights go out completely. Instrumental version of Go
to Dark Gethsemane in the darkness. Quietly the choir
members come in and strip the sanctuary of all linens
and décor, including candles. After they have finished,*
VERONICA, *wearing a white nurse's outfit comes in and*

kneels to pray. PASTOR *comes in, pursued by* NORBERT, *who wears a dark suit.)*

NORBERT: *(Putting something he's carrying out of sight, then turning on the lights.)* Pastor, you don't have that kind of money! She'll probably buy grain alcohol or crack!

PASTOR: I'm not here to judge her. If she needs it she needs it. I don't know what she needs. I don't know who she is.

NORBERT:	PASTOR:
(Adjusting the lights)	God knows her.
Funny, I always thought	God knows what
Pastors knew what	she needs.
everybody needed deep	
down. Think of all the	
time and effort I put into	
these lights and now….	

*(*VERONICA *disappears.)*

(Overlapping NORBERT. *Coming in with* LOTTIE. *Both wear dark clothes.)*

YOLANDA: No, I'm not upset. I just always thought she liked my voice better. No offense.

LOTTIE: She wanted to give me a good start on my new career. Since I won't be needed at Mount Olive.

PASTOR: I bet the office manager at Mount Olive can't help out with Hebrew translations.

*(*LARRY *comes in, also in a dark suit.* YOLANDA, *studiously ignoring him, turns back to* LOTTIE. VERONICA *reappears with a Tupperware container of treats.)*

YOLANDA: What are you singing?

LOTTIE: *Be Still.*

YOLANDA: I *said* no offense.

PASTOR: The song.

(VERONICA *leaves with the Tupperware.*)

LOTTIE: *(Overlapping* PASTOR*)* The song *Be Still.* That's what I'm singing.

YOLANDA: Oh. That old thing.

LOTTIE: She liked it. Especially when I sang it.

YOLANDA: You have the breath control for the pianissimo?

PASTOR: We're all getting a chance to sing for her, Yolanda.

YOLANDA: As a *group.*

PASTOR: Well, you know, I've long felt that we never sounded all that good as individuals—

(VERONICA *reappears without the Tupperware. She starts sorting through sheet music.*)

YOLANDA: I'm professionally trained! I've spent a lot of money—

LARRY: That's for sure.

PASTOR: Of course, there are voices of distinction. But mostly we're just volunteers who like to sing—no one's ever going to pay us. Yet when we all sing together, when we really listen to each other, when we blend, and watch Peter, we sound surprisingly wonderful.

NORBERT: That happens every Sunday in every church around the world.

PASTOR: I don't think so, not like this. *(Gets teary)* Not even in France. Not even Taize.

LARRY: Now, don't everybody be sad. This is a milestone!

YOLANDA: It's a *funeral.*

LARRY: Right. Of course. But—I mean—today—it's the beginning of a bigger, better, stronger congregation—

YOLANDA: Sounds like an ad for 24-Hour Fitness.

LARRY: The endowment will provide almost a third of the operating budget for Mount Olive. And when we all start going there on a regular basis, the attendance will double—so will the offering. Think of all the social outreach—we could expand Hospice in Home—that's a terrific program—!

NORBERT: Um…I think—

PASTOR: Larry—

LOTTIE: It's a funeral!

LARRY: You're right. I'm sorry. I'm sad, too. But she wouldn't want us to be. We're celebrating a life.

YOLANDA: *That* sounds like an ad for Forest Lawn.

NORBERT: I'm glad she wanted the service here, rather than at Mount Olive.

PASTOR: The last service held at Orange Grove.

PETER: *(Coming in, dressed in a dark suit)* Good afternoon, everyone.

EVERYONE: *(Variously)* Hello, Peter. Good afternoon.

PETER: Before everyone else gets here, Lottie, do you want to go over your solo?

LOTTIE: Nope. I've got it! I'm a professional.

PASTOR: As of today.

PETER: *(To LARRY)* And how are we today, O Destroyer of Churches?

PASTOR: Peter—

PETER: O Pillager of Historical Landmarks—

(PASTOR *leaves.*)

LARRY: It's not historical—

PETER: O Layer to Waste of the Spiritual Realm!

LARRY: I'm sorry they won't take you on at Mount Olive.

PETER: O Vanquisher of Music!

LARRY: I didn't think they'd only want the one organist.

PETER: There's only one organ, Larry. An *electric* organ! And one organist. And one service on Sundays. So that one organist will get a raise—thanks to your endowment. Go on—wreak your havoc!

LARRY: Maybe this means you can finish at U S C.

YOLANDA: He's too old, Larry. He's never going to finish.

LARRY: Not here, Yolanda.

PETER: I'm *not* gonna finish. Can't afford it. I'll just… stay on at the hospital and volunteer to accompany musicals in community theatre. I'll be that guy who gets drunk at parties and plays *Send in the Clowns*.

LARRY: But you're a great organist!

PETER: Maybe, but I'm tired. This will be a good break.

LARRY: You're tired cause of your job. That hospital sucks it out of you. I need an office manager—

YOLANDA: You don't have an office.

LARRY: A business manager, an administrator—that's what you do at the hospital, isn't it? Administrate?

PETER: Yes, but—

LARRY: I could pay you better than a non-profit and it wouldn't be hard at all. Part time—

PETER: No—

LARRY: Give you a chance to compose—

PETER: No, Larry. I can't.

LARRY: Why not?

PETER: It's just too…I don't need to make a lot of money. I'm Lutheran. I'd feel guilty.

(PASTOR *returns from the sacristy wearing his ceremonial vestments.*)

LARRY: That's what's wrong with Lutherans! Always trying to stay pure by rejecting the world—that's why Lutheran churches are in decline, always struggling—

LOTTIE: Hello, I'm not Lutheran. And I'm out of a job.

(VERONICA *finishes with the music and disappears.*)

PASTOR: (*Handing the U-curve to* NORBERT) There's nothing wrong with struggling.

NORBERT: It's all we know. I probably won't even join Mount Olive. Their building's so new nothing needs fixing. (*Leaves*)

LARRY: But if you're not struggling, if you're comfortable, you can help other people—like a church is supposed to!

PASTOR: But that's when churches get in trouble, when they're comfortable. The Roman church—that's when Luther left. A church is a sanctuary to the homeless and the broken, so it's okay if it's a little broken, too. Not a triumphant altar to glory, but to frailty.

LARRY: But we're worshipping God….

PASTOR: In the guise of humanity.

LOTTIE: Speaking of frailty, who took Simon to the hospital?

PASTOR: Oh, I think Norbert did.

PETER: Pastor, where is he going to go? They're not going to let him live in Mount Olive.

(NORBERT *returns with some music.)*

LARRY: He'll go into a shelter, where he can get some real rehabilitation.

PASTOR: He wouldn't go before. Now there's no choice.

NORBERT: We weren't doing him any good here. Just giving him handouts. No motivation.

YOLANDA: Aren't *we* warm and loving!

LOTTIE: Who said that? Miss Congeniality?

(NORBERT *abruptly leaves.)*

PETER: We failed him. One quiet cataclysm after another.

LARRY: I wouldn't talk about warm and loving if I were you—

PASTOR: I hope you all will come visit me at Taize.

YOLANDA: Do they let women visit?

PASTOR: It's a religious community, but not a monastery.

LARRY: I don't understand why you have to go. We're going to need your help settling everyone in over at Mount Olive.

PETER: It's a synod rule.

PASTOR: Actually, it's a churchwide rule. At least in the U S.

LARRY: Pastors have to leave the country when—when they—?

PASTOR: Retiring pastors—and that's what I'm doing, I suppose—retiring pastors are strongly urged not to stay involved at their former churches.

LARRY: That's not right.

PASTOR: No, it's a good idea. Retired pastors sometimes meddle—

LARRY: You wouldn't.

PASTOR: I'd try not to. But parishioners have a tendency to "consult" with the former pastor if he's around. Very difficult for the new minister. It's a smart idea for me to say *au revoir.*

YOLANDA: And you love France.

PASTOR: *Mais oui!*

YOLANDA: *Moi aussi.* So can I come visit?

PASTOR:
I'll be at Taize most of the time, but I'll make plenty of excursions, so don't just drop in unannounced.

NORBERT:
(Coming back in)
I don't suppose they'll need another baptismal font at Mount Olive. Ours is much nicer. Maybe we could sell it on eBay.

YOLANDA: Of course not.

PASTOR: But you're welcome any time I'm there.

YOLANDA: Where will you go first?

(VERONICA reappears, and sits quietly, listening.)

PETER: Back to Chartres?

PASTOR: Well, now there's an idea. I have a little mission to accomplish there.

NORBERT: Oh, that's right.

LARRY: What's that?

PETER: Pastor always told me to go to the cathedral at Chartres, so when I finally saved enough money to go to Paris, I took the train out to the country. It was dark and quiet inside the church, very medieval. I walked down the center aisle, over the inlaid stone maze and around the ambulatory until I was directly behind the altar. Then I reached into a secret niche and pulled out a note—addressed to me. It said, "Dear Peter: Welcome to wonderful Chartres. Light a candle for someone you love."

LARRY: It was from Pastor?

PASTOR: I always visit Chartres.

PETER: So I wrote a note and stuffed it back in the secret niche. "Dear Pastor: You said light a candle for someone you love, so I lit one for you."

PASTOR: Thank you.

(Sound of a chainsaw outside)

YOLANDA:What's that?

LOTTIE: It's the Orange Grove Chainsaw Massacre!

LARRY: They're not supposed to come till tomorrow—

PASTOR	NORBERT
Who?	Who's they?

LARRY: Some of the demolition people—

YOLANDA:	NORBERT
We're still using the church!	I'm still chair of Property Management!

LARRY: Not for the church—

PETER:	NORBERT:
The orange tree!	A little disrespectful, don't
(Runs out)	you think?

(Over her shoulder to LARRY as she dashes out after PETER:)

LOTTIE: Why didn't you let me schedule this?

YOLANDA: Good going, champ.

LARRY: This was scheduled before the funeral—I forgot—

YOLANDA:	NORBERT
Then go out and tell them to stop—for Pastor's sake!	Fine, do what you want. *(Leaves)*

PASTOR: Really for Gustafina's.

LARRY: Oh, man, I'm sorry—how dumb can I get? *(Dashes out. Yelling at the workmen)* Hey! Hold off a minute—!

YOLANDA: Are you all right?

PASTOR: It's just a tree. The fruit's been sour for years.

YOLANDA: But if we dug around the roots, put on some manure—

(The sound of the chainsaw ceases.)

PASTOR: *(Smiles)* Too late, don't you think?

YOLANDA: Not even one more year to see if the fruit sweetens?

PASTOR: Even Jesus would chop it down now.

YOLANDA: I grew up in this church. And sometimes I hated it. Especially during—

PASTOR: Confirmation class?

YOLANDA: Was I that bad?

PASTOR: You used to put on eyeshadow during Luther's Small Catechism.

YOLANDA: Mount Olive has terrible acoustics. I went over there on Saturday and tried *Ave Maria*, the Schubert—

PASTOR: Careful, they don't like Latin over there. Pastor Thronson does an annual Kick the Pope sermon.

YOLANDA: I got accepted for Master Chorale.

PASTOR: L A Master Chorale? At the Music Center?

(YOLANDA nods, not exactly humbly.)

PASTOR: Congratulations.

YOLANDA: So I think that's where I'll be singing from now on.

PASTOR: I understand.

YOLANDA: And things with Larry would be...still kind of—

PASTOR: Uncomfortable. Of course.

YOLANDA: I'm happy, in a weird way—

PASTOR: About Mastor Chorale? It's wonderful!

YOLANDA: No, more like a weight's been lifted—

YOLANDA & PASTOR: —Relief! *(They both laugh.)*

PASTOR: *(Looking outside)* Oh, look.

YOLANDA: Gustafina.

PASTOR: Looks pretty good, doesn't she?

YOLANDA: Well, considering—

NORBERT: *(Coming in supporting a very unsteady* GUSTAFINA *on his arm)* Look who I found!

*(*VERONICA *stands up, expectant.)*

PASTOR: *(Going to her)* Gustafina! You look terrific!

(In fact, GUSTAFINA *looks pretty frail. She's limping and apparently doesn't have the use of one hand.)*

YOLANDA: How are you feeling?

GUSTAFINA: Much—much—um—um—

YOLANDA: Better?

GUSTAFINA: *(Nodding)* Ja.

PASTOR: It's wonderful you could make it today.

GUSTAFINA: I—must—important!

YOLANDA: Veronica would be glad you're here.

PASTOR: She is.

*(*VERONICA *smiles.)*

NORBERT: *(Trying to lead* GUSTAFINA *to a seat.)*

Come sit, so you can listen—

GUSTAFINA: *(Resisting)* No—

NORBERT: Just a few steps—

GUSTAFINA: No—I can—can—want to—sing!

(The others look at each other doubtfully.)

PASTOR: In that case we won't process. Why don't you sit in your usual place?

GUSTAFINA: *Ja.*

(With NORBERT'S *help* GUSTAFINA *takes her usual place next to* VERONICA.*)*

LARRY: *(Rushing in)* I stopped them for now. They won't cut down the—

YOLANDA: Larry, quiet! Look who's here.

LARRY: Gustafina! You look great! Considering…

GUSTAFINA: *Danke schön.*

(Coming in with LOTTIE:*)*

PETER: Larry, send them home.

LOTTIE: They won't go.

LARRY:
They can wait a little bit, but it's been scheduled— it'll cost too much to postpone—

PETER: We're having a funeral here!

NORBERT:
Somebody gets a little authority…! Not his place at all! *I'm* Property Management—I don't care if he *is* President!

YOLANDA: They can't knock down the church with us in it!

PASTOR: Now, everyone, it's not like we don't have another church.

PETER: NORBERT:
What? Move the whole   I'm just a little bit furious.
funeral over to—?

PASTOR: —To Mount Olive.

YOLANDA: Honestly!

LOTTIE: I've got people coming to hear me sing.

PASTOR: A lot of people are coming. Not to worry. We can leave someone here to direct them to Mount Olive. Lottie, please call the funeral home so they can redirect the hearse.

(LOTTIE *whips out a cell phone and disappears.*)

PETER: Can we at least practice here? Will they give us that much time?

LARRY: I guess so, they're taking a break. I'm so, so sorry about this.

PASTOR: That's all right, Larry. Don't worry about it.

NORBERT: I think he *should* worry about it! Decisions have been made—important decisions—without proper consideration! We used to make decisions together, with *some* input from the Property Management Committee. That's how we decided on the organ, the altar—do you understand? Does everybody understand
how this building works,   PETER:
how every part means   Norbert—
something?

LOTTIE: *(Coming back in)* They're diverting to Mount Olive.

NORBERT: *(Going to the altar)* The nave is like an upside-down ship. The altar—do you remember when we changed it?

PASTOR: LOTTIE:
Oh, yes, Norbert, you did   *That* decision was a long

a wonderful job!   time coming! And
                                    construction took *forever.*

NORBERT: (*Demonstrating*) It used to be a tomb altar,
flat against the wall, so for communion Pastor had to
face away from the congregation. But I cut it in half—
very delicate, and yes, it did take me a while—then I
moved the front half forward so now it's a table altar
and Pastor faces us when he blesses the sacraments. It
made a big difference and nobody even remembers, I
bet!

PASTOR: Of course, we do, Norbert.

NORBERT: And now it's just going to be dismantled!

PETER: The organ, too, Norbert, but we need to
practice.

NORBERT: I'm sorry, I'm sorry. I'm kinda aggravated.

PETER: We're all tense, but we're running out of time.

(*Settling in at the piano as* NORBERT *returns to his place:*)

PETER: Okay, everyone. Let's be perfect the first time
so we can get on over to Mount Olive before the roof
caves in here.

NORBERT: Which is it, please?

PETER: (*Holds up music*) Veronica's favorite.

GUSTAFINA: *Ja.*

NORBERT: Oh, mine too. At least something's going my
way.

(PETER *gives pitches and they sing a capella. They are, in
fact, perfect.*)

EVERYONE: (*Except* VERONICA. *Singing in harmony*)
Thine is the glory, risen conquering Son
Endless is the victory thou o'er death hast won

(GUSTAFINA *is singing just fine, and the others look at her
in amazement, gradually dropping out one by one to listen.*)

EVERYONE: *(Except* VERONICA*)*
Angels in bright raiment rolled the stone away

(Finally everyone is listening except GUSTAFINA, *who sings with great ardor [she can't hear that the others have stopped].)*

GUSTAFINA:
Kept the folded grave clothes where thy body lay

EVERYONE: *(Except* VERONICA. *Happily joining* GUSTAFINA *for the last lines)*
Thine is the glory, risen conquering Son
Endless is the victory thou o'er death hast won.

PETER: Wonderful, everyone. You sound—we sound—
(Almost surprised) —Really, really good.

LOTTIE: Wow. You never compliment us.

PETER: I do, too, all the time!

NORBERT: But this time he means it.

PETER:	PASTOR:
I always mean it!	You *did* sound a little shocked.

PETER:	LARRY:
Never mind!	Well, now you've ruined it.

GUSTAFINA: *(In German) Was? Was? (What? What?)*

PETER: Gustafina, you did a marvelous job of holding up the alto line by yourself.

YOLANDA: *(Almost under her breath, but not quite)*
Because she was singing the melody....

GUSTAFINA: *Danke schön.* I—for—for—Velomint—

YOLANDA & NORBERT: Veronica.

GUSTAFINA: *Ja.*

PASTOR: We do throw a good funeral.

NORBERT: We ought to—we spend our whole lives preparing for it.

PETER: All religions are death cults.

(Everyone stares at PETER.*)*

PETER: Sorry.

NORBERT: We did sound good. Even with people missing.

YOLANDA: Maybe that's why we sound good.

(Everyone stares at YOLANDA.*)*

YOLANDA: Sorry. *(To* LOTTIE*)* We blended well, I thought.

PETER:	LOTTIE:
We should head on out.	*(Astonished)*
	Thank you.

PASTOR: Who can stay to direct people to Mount Olive?

NORBERT: I will.

PETER: No, no, we need you all there. We can't afford any more missing voices.

NORBERT: I can make a sign.

PASTOR: That will have to do.

NORBERT: *(Going to the door)* I'll just post it on the front door like the 95 Theses. Oh, wait, can't forget this.

(Produces a white mound on a large platter.)

YOLANDA: Bread cake!

NORBERT: Veronica's layer loaf for the reception. The recipe will live on.

LOTTIE:	YOLANDA:	PETER:
I can't have any—	I'm lactose	I'm dieting this
it's not kosher.	intolerant.	week.

*(*PASTOR *glares.)*

LOTTIE:	YOLANDA:	PETER:
But maybe I can make an exception—*today*.	But I have some pills.	But I suppose a taste won't hurt....

(VERONICA *looks pleased.*)

NORBERT: (*As the doorknob comes off in his hand*) Oh, dear. I knew that was going to happen eventually. (*Trying to shove the doorknob back in*) Came right off in my hand. Give me a minute. I think I can—

PETER: We don't have a minute. I'm going to get the last of my music and I want the rest of you there before I arrive!

(GUSTAFINA, LOTTIE, YOLANDA, *and* LARRY *start toward the door.* PETER *goes out through a different door to get music.*)

PASTOR: It's all right, Norbert. We won't be using it.

NORBERT: (*Dropping the doorknob on the floor*) You're right. Why worry about it? We're free, in a sense. This building's a money pit. (*He struggles to get the door open.*) As soon as I—

LARRY: Here, Norbert.

NORBERT: No, I don't need any—!

(*As* LARRY *helps him get the door open:*)

NORBERT: There. (*He goes out.*)

LOTTIE: (*With a handful of bulletins*) Guess we don't need these any more either. (*Carelessly drops them. They scatter. She leaves.*)

YOLANDA: (*Helping* GUSTAFINA *to the door*) I can drive you, Gustafina, unless you want to go with Norbert.

GUSTAFINA: (*Tries to say something, can't find the word*) Ja.

YOLANDA: *Ja* what? You want to go with me or Norbert?

GUSTAFINA: *Ja.*

(GUSTAFINA *goes out with* YOLANDA.)

LARRY: Pastor, you need a ride?

PASTOR: Oh, no. I've got vestments and things in my car. Mount Olive might as well have them.

LARRY: That'll be good. Some continuity.

(Sees PETER *coming back in with music:)*

LARRY: See you there. *(Disappears.)*

PETER: Boy, he took off.

PASTOR: You told him to get out of here.

PETER: As always, not quite enough time to do it right. And where's Simon?

PASTOR: I'm not tenor enough for you?

PETER: Oh, yeah, Norbert took him to the hospital—

PASTOR: —The loony bin.

PETER: Really, the loony bin?

PASTOR: The hospital, but the mental ward. I made arrangements, Lottie helped. He finally agreed to go, but only if Norbert drove him.

PETER: Did he just—tump over the edge?

PASTOR: He'd balanced there for a long time.

PETER: Did he hurt himself?

PASTOR: Change is not...he doesn't—

PETER: None of us do. *(Busily organizing music)* France. That'll be nice. Taize's pretty?

PASTOR: Very nice. *(After a moment)* Peter.

PETER: Pastor?

PASTOR: Say something to Larry.

PETER: Say…what kind of something?

PASTOR: He's not with Yolanda any more.

PETER: *(Sits at the organ, plays quietly)* Pastor, don't be ridiculous. Nobody's more— *(Struggles for the word, won't say it)* —Than Larry, and nobody's less— *(A different struggle)* —Than he is either. He offered me a job. It would be horrible.

PASTOR: Really? A job? Hmmm.

PETER: Stop.

PASTOR: He didn't offer Lottie a job. Take it.

PETER: If he asks again—

PASTOR: We're too cautious, don't you think? I've been driving my whole life with hands at ten and two. Careful, prudent, not necessarily with money, but with people's feelings at least.

PETER: That's your job.

PASTOR: But is it yours?

PETER: Isn't it everybody's?

PASTOR: Well—

PASTOR & PETER: —Lutherans, anyway. *(They laugh.)*

PASTOR: What would Veronica say?

PETER: She'd push me. She'd make fun of me. Please don't do that.

PASTOR: And you're above love.

PETER: Don't!

PASTOR: What else do you have going on? Really?

(PETER says nothing.)

PASTOR: There. I wasn't careful with your feelings. Maybe we *are* free now.

PETER: That sounds so awful. I can't believe you let it—we let it—seems like we just bought the organ—what a waste. It all happened fast, didn't it?

PASTOR: Like a thief in the night.

PETER: *(Shutting off the organ)* Wish I could take this home.

PASTOR: You'll find a church.

PETER: So will you.

PASTOR: Maybe. But I don't know if I'd fit in anywhere else. Orange Grove Lutheran is pretty unique.

PETER: You're way too young to retire. You can't just give up. We all depend on you. You were *called*.

PASTOR: I think now I'm *called away*.

PETER: Veronica depended on you. She admired you very much, you know.

PASTOR: *(Surprised and delighted)* Admired me? Really?

PETER: Very much.

(VERONICA turns away, embarrassed.)

PASTOR: Oh, my!

LARRY: *(Coming back in)* Pastor, Gustafina wants you.

PASTOR: Of course.

(Starts to leave, LARRY starts to go with him.)

PASTOR: Can you help Peter? *(He disappears.)*

LARRY: What do you need?

PETER: Nothing. I don't know why he said that. *(Indicating the music in his hands)* It's just music.

(They stand there awkwardly for a moment.)

PETER: When the churches merge, will you be president?

LARRY: They want me to. But I don't know.

PETER: *(Shrugs)* I'm sure you could. There's that endowment to manage.

LARRY: I won't know anybody there.

(VERONICA stands, as if hopeful.)

PETER: Oh, sure. *Some* people from here will go there. *(Pause)* I wouldn't know anyone either. *(Pause)* And their choirmaster *prefers* his electronic organ.

LARRY: Gloomy day. For a funeral.

PETER: Marine layer.

LARRY: When I was a kid they used to call it June Swoon or June Gloom. But—global warming—now it starts in April and goes all the way to August. Maybe someday L A will be a rainforest instead of a desert.

PETER: I'd like to believe in that—warming theory—but—

LARRY: No?

PETER: The universe is getting colder, not hotter.

LARRY: Now how do you figure *that*?

PETER: Expanding, spreading out, farther apart—makes sense to me—as much as anything does. *(Shrugs)*

LARRY: *(Nodding)* Colder.

(Sound of the chainsaw again.)

LARRY: What are they—? They're supposed to—
(Dashes out)

(PETER stares after LARRY for a moment, then quickly engrosses himself in sorting his music. VERONICA relaxes—sadly—and watches him. He looks at his watch, goes to the door, starts to leave, then steps back inside. The chainsaw sound ceases. GUSTAFINA comes in on PASTOR'S arm, still limping.)

PASTOR: Gustafina wanted one last look.

GUSTAFINA: *Mein kinder—wasser—*watered, no—wet—

PETER: Baptized? They were all baptized here?

GUSTAFINA: *Ja.*

PASTOR: Peter—?

PETER: *Guten Erinerrungen,* Frau Liedtke?

PASTOR: *(Indicating* LARRY) Did—?

PETER: Please!

GUSTAFINA: *Mein Ehemann—die Bestattung—*

PETER: Pastor Liedtke had his funeral here.

PASTOR: I officiated.

PETER: Oh! Hold on a minute! *(Disappears)*

GUSTAFINA: *Schön. Schön! (Starts to cry)*

PASTOR: Gustafina, you know I don't know any German. *Parle-tu français?*

GUSTAFINA: *Die Bestattung—*

PASTOR: Does that mean "funeral?"

PETER: *(Returning with a small white box)* "*Bestattung*" is funeral, yes.

GUSTAFINA: *Schön.*

PETER: *(Handing her the box)* Did you want—Pastor Liedtke...?

PASTOR: Oh, Peter, no—

GUSTAFINA: *(Accepting the box)* Bitte. Danke.

PETER: *Schön.*

PASTOR: Oh, dear. What will we do with the others? We can't leave them here. It's probably even illegal.

GUSTAFINA: *Schön.*

(Taking GUSTAFINA *out:)*

PETER: A beautiful service. I'm sure it was.

GUSTAFINA: *(As they leave) Schön…*

(PASTOR is left alone with VERONICA. She watches him, but he can't see her. He looks around the room, perhaps for the last time. He picks up the bulletins that LOTTIE scattered earlier. He leaves and closes the door behind him. Just as the door is closing, SIMON gropes his way in from another door. SIMON is grubbier than before, his hair has gotten long, and his beard has come in quite a bit.)

SIMON: *(Feebly)* Good morning, everyone! I've had all my pills now. Every single one. Every single one…is gone. Pastor? Yolanda? *(Tries the door. Finds there is no knob.)* Hey! I'm coming, too!

(The sound of the chainsaw begins again outside.)

SIMON: Open up! You're gonna need me there! They don't have nobody like me! *(Bangs on the door)* Who's gonna watch out for things? Someone's gotta watch— *(Staggers, dizzy)* Whoa! *(Sits down abruptly)* Someone's gotta…give me a ride. I can stay for a little bit, and watch for a while, but I can't forever.

(VERONICA goes to SIMON and lays her hands gently on him. He does not notice.)

SIMON: They're gonna tear this place down in three days. But there's still a lotta…stuff here…and somebody's gotta watch it. All kindsa people come here, and they're not all…good people. All kinds of temptation. I'm ready! Won't anyone…watch with me? Can no one— *(Curling up)* —Stay…?

(The strange musical sigh is heard once again. SIMON falls asleep with VERONICA watching over him. The sound of the chainsaw gets louder.)

END OF PLAY